JESUS
IN
PINK

RESTORING THE POWER OF HER
KINGDOM BLUEPRINT

Tamera Vallejo, MBA

100% Creator Designed

"I cannot recommend this book highly enough. It's not just a book for women; it's a must-read for anyone who has ever uttered the words, 'I just want to know my purpose and what God wants me to do.' After finishing this book, I feel incredibly empowered to take the structured blueprint it offers and begin filling the gaps in my quest to discover my identity, purpose, assignment, and calling. Tammy has not only validated many of my personal experiences as a woman in leadership, Corporate America, and the church, but she has also given a much-needed voice to women and a language to articulate how to navigate when we embrace our roles in both the church and our culture. I encourage you to gift yourself with these profound truths and principles. Embark on this healing journey and unlock the unique gifts, plans, and purposes that have been specially crafted for you by our loving Father God."

Kim Canright
Director of Operations

"As a friend, peer and witness to Tamera's story and her reconciliation journey, I am grateful that she has been obedient to Jesus by putting it in writing for others to see. As she walked out this very personal journey, she always kept her eyes on Jesus and intentionally responded to every situation with integrity and a desire to only do what the Father said to do. *Jesus in Pink* validates the thoughts we keep to ourselves as we move in the purposes Jesus has for us as women, while also providing a valuable toolbox of experience to lean on as you walk in your own Jesus purpose."

Suzanne Glassman
Founder/CEO Morning star Entertainment

"God created man and woman and generously gives both spiritual gifts. Why don't we celebrate the giftings of both equally? Women have been underserved within the body of Christ for far too long, and Tammy's work clearly highlights the Church's shortcomings in this conversation. Romans 12:2 tells us not to copy the behaviors and customs of this world and Tammy shows us where scripture and the church have drifted apart on this topic. *Jesus in Pink* lays out an easy-to-follow timeline of Tammy's experiences within the Church and what God taught her about how He values women. I believe this work will help men and women gain a more complete biblical perspective of God's creation and the role each of us plays within His divine rescue plan."

Jim Brangenberg
Co-host of iWork4Him, sheWorks4Him, and iWork4Him Power Thoughts

"Jesus in Pink is such a refreshing gift to me and the many women who will read it. Tammy Vallejo has used her experiences to uncover lies and expose God's truth about women. Thank you, Tammy for doing the hard work that I have failed even to consider. Your writings have taught me so much about the limiting beliefs of not only women but the Holy Spirit. Your authentic, personal approach gives credibility to your story and allows God to use you to shine a light on a tough subject. Your goal to unite the church around this subject is near and dear to my heart and a much-needed aspect of the conversation. Thank you for stewarding this subject so well."

Martha Brangenberg
Co-host of iWork4Him, sheWorks4Him, and iWork4Him Power Thoughts

"Jesus in Pink is a journey. Tammy is candid about the difficult and often hurtful things she has endured as a woman both in the realm of business and the church. But *Jesus in Pink* doesn't stop there. Tammy also takes you on her healing journey with God and what He says about the pink side of His creation: you. *Jesus in Pink* is about re-establishing God's Divine blueprint for His people whom He loves. My hope for *Jesus in Pink* is that it will heal women and set them free to pursue their Divine calling. And then, to extend that same freedom and healing to all others, in the church, in business, and in the world."

Whitney Stadtman
Author, Speaker, Producer *Raising the Remnant* Podcast

"If anyone has the experience and authority to write a book on this topic then it is Tammy. I've seen her walk out the process of everything she teaches with such authenticity, humility, and even sincerity. If you, like many of us women called to lead, have been impacted by the lies and schemes of the enemy to steal our God-given identity and our unique voice then this book is for you!"

Kathleen Bahm
Mom, Wife, Prayer and Deliverance Minister

JESUS IN PINK

RESTORING THE POWER OF HER
KINGDOM BLUEPRINT

Tamera Vallejo, MBA

JESUS IN PINK MEDIA

Jesus in Pink: Restoring the Power of Her Kingdom Blueprint

Printed in the United States of America
Library of Congress Cataloging-in-Publication Data
Library of Congress Control Number: 2023920953

FIRST EDITION

Tamera Vallejo–1st ed.
TITLE: Jesus in Pink: Restoring the Power of Her Kingdom Blueprint
ISBN–13 Paperback: 979-8-9889387-8-1
Hardcover: 979-8-9889387-0-5
eBook: 979-8-9889387-1-2

1. REL012130 Religion/Christian Living/Women's Interests
2. RELIGION/Leadership/Spirituality

My family, including my husband and best friend Tom and our son-in-law, Kyle, who are the best examples of how to truly love and honor women, our daughters, Gabby, Karly, and Alyssa, who lived this journey with us and are amazing women despite the challenges of the journey. And to our grandchildren who will carry the legacy of Jesus into future generations.

Contents

INTRODUCTION

I didn't recognize who I was anymore. For the first time in my life, I had no titles, no purpose, no vision, and no businesses to define me. I was exhausted, crushed in spirit, and questioning everything I believed and thought I had heard from God. Though I was raised in the Church and am a woman gifted in leadership, business, and entrepreneurship, I struggled to know where I fit in God's plan. I never felt like I fit the mold of the church, and I had no context for what it would be like to move into ministry. But I wanted the big assignment from God, and I believed that meant I had to do it in the church, or at least *with* the church. I wasn't sure how God would reconcile the limiting belief system that I had been taught most churches held about women, namely remaining silent and not being allowed to lead in the church, but I assumed if God was asking me to do it, he would work all of that out. I wrote this book for those of you who do not feel the freedom to be who God designed you to be, either in the church or in culture, and are wondering if you are part of God's plan, especially if you are a woman in leadership and passionate about Jesus. We've whispered under our breath together, shared our frustrations, rolled our eyes at the comments, and sometimes even advances of some of the men, cried together when the promotion didn't come our way, and we've sat in churches knowing God didn't wire us to be "less than" the men, second in position, or silent. And we did these things, accepting what we were taught, all the while praying, hoping, and dreaming things would change.

One morning in September 2021 I woke up and Jesus met me in a vision. He said, "I know you have been writing a book on unity in the Church and that's important, but I need you to put it down and write a different book first. Unity cannot happen until my daughter's step into position." I debated the merits of this seemingly abrupt shift and rather childishly said to Him, "Fine then, but you are going to need to name it and write it because I don't have anything else left in me." I jumped in the shower, and the audible voice of God said to me, "The name of the book is *Jesus in Pink*. I giggled, and then I had a long cry. I needed to know in that moment that Jesus did and does represent, stand for, walk with, defend, advocate for, and would march with women—*today*, if He were here.

Only God knew the details of every horrendous story over my lifetime where I had reached the pinnacle of leadership, many times as the only woman in the room, only to be shut down and denied the top positions because I was a woman. And only He knew the depth of the tears, frustration, and anger that I experienced as I picked myself up time after time to restart and forge forward on the next new path, hoping it would be different. And only He knew that I had resolved in 2009 to do things His way and go "all in" on His plans as I shifted my gaze from business to ministry, trusting Him with the outcome, only to find myself in the same fetal position I had found myself before, only this time it felt like it was directed by Him, instead of a man. I didn't know on that September morning in 2021 exactly how God was going to reconcile my journey as a woman in His church or how He would ask me to write it, but I knew I was uniquely qualified on the subject, and it had to mean He had a plan to restore women and shift His Church.

I wrote this book at God's prompting to share the journey and corresponding process—the PINK framework—that God took me through to restore me back to His original design and to help me see His blueprint for me and my place in His Church again. As you begin your own journey, on your own timeline, you too will not only experience God's restoration of your life, but you will also gain an understanding of how you fit in His plan. Each chapter heading represents God restoring His power in the order and progression that He did for me, while bringing healing to some very broken parts of me and my journey, and empowering and restoring me to lead in His church. That process not only resulted in me finally being able to walk in peace and freedom in my feminine identity, purpose, leadership, and calling, but I have also engaged with many women since who have experienced this process with similar results. My hope is that you will not only take this journey with God yourself, but that you will also take others on it with you in your homes, organizations, and churches.

The longest part of the journey for me was accepting the evidence that God revealed to me along the way, learning to depend on the Holy Spirit to guide me, and allowing God's enduring and inclusive love to empower me, even when the world that sometimes-included people in the Church, did not. I had believed so many lies about God for over forty years! My prayer is that having all the resources in one place here will help you have a more efficient journey than mine, in discovering how God really designed women, and how His design includes us in His plan, including in leadership in the Church. Ephesians 4:14 says, "Then we will no longer be infants, tossed back and forth by the waves, and blown here and there by every wind of teaching and by the cunning and craftiness of people in their deceitful scheming." If you get to the end of this book and you still believe that leadership in churches should only be held by men, like I did, that is okay. It is a viable interpretation of Scripture and not the point of the book. But the expansion of that belief to justify a whole host of abuses against women and daughters, eroding and disrupting their feminine identity, purpose, leadership and calling, is not only not okay, it is inconsistent with God's design and what He says in Scripture, both for men and women.

As God takes you through this process as He did me, some of your perceptions will change and your own frustration with the limited belief system, will turn to peace as He heals you, but it is a process. God never intended for you and other women, or men for that matter, to sit on the sidelines or be second. He designed us all to be part of His plan and He calls us all into a purpose designed specifically for us to walk out with Him. But when that design is disrupted, and we lose ourselves to the enemy's schemes and strategies, and sometimes our connection to God as well, that's not part of His design. God is restoring women and He's shifting His church to honor your calling, both inside of and outside of the church. It's time to discover and become established in your own Prophetic identity, Incubated purpose, Nurtured leadership, and Kingdom calling, and restore your power in Him. Are you ready?

CHAPTER 1

THE POWER OF HER JOURNEY

"For I know the plans I have for you,' declares the
LORD, 'plans to prosper you and not to harm
you, plans to give you hope and a future."

—JEREMIAH 29:11

The power of your journey is being able to take the challenges and failures life offers you and using them to level up into a better place than you were before. As we begin this journey together, I want you to know this book is written so that you will not only see yourself in the pages but also experience and learn from others' stories, both my own and those of other women who have overcome some horrendous things. Most women I meet don't want to spend a lot of time recounting or reliving their stories, because it is often too painful and maybe even still triggering to do so. At the same time, we're all in a moment in time when our journeys can influence others by becoming one voice to shape culture, not just for us but for those who will come after us.

Your unique journey in life not only shapes you but your family, friends, and others you meet along the way. And because we all have free will to make our own choices in life, the journey will include both good and bad experiences. The real question is, Will your journey empower you or leave you debilitated? It's designed to empower you into your calling as you lean on Jesus for direction, restoration, and reconciliation along the way. But if your journey gets disrupted either by your own choices or the choices of others, especially by a traumatic event or experiences that are out of your control, it can change the course of your life in both positive and negative ways. This seems to be more so the case for women than for men, and it's hard to understand why God doesn't always intervene. But He wants to reconcile your experiences and help you see that He was always there with you even when things were hard. And He wants to restore you to the person He always knew you would be, which sometimes takes looking in the rearview mirror to see it from a different lens than when you were in it. And it is that look back that will point you to the evidence that will both completely heal you and equip you to move forward in your authentic identity and calling, as your journey becomes your testimony.

I have always been wired to lead, even when I didn't want to. If you're a leader, you understand what I'm talking about. And with leadership, there are always challenges. One of the challenges that has often been a part of my journey, has been having to overcome a belief system in culture that women should stay silent, let the men lead regardless of gifting, stay in the home, and not work. And unfortunately, because I was born in the 1960's, my journey has paralleled many of the cultural social changes that have progressed for women since then. As a result, many women in my age group have multiple stories that we commiserate over at times. Some of my stories were so part of the landscape, they don't seem shocking to me anymore, but I'll warn you they are.

The big assignment God had given me was to unite His Church, and He gave me a blueprint on how to do it, first instructing me to develop community-based projects that no church could accomplish alone. With my entrepreneurial mind-set and experience as a business leader, not only was this attainable, but I thought I knew how to do it. In 2009, I founded a church nonprofit organization that would unite churches in our City around innovative strategies to social issues and I hit the road running. I developed a board and a team, and we quickly started building initiatives that would address homelessness, sex trafficking and poverty in underserved areas, and partnered with people in churches and the community. In 2013, we expanded the ministry and opened a co-working space and kingdom business incubator focused on helping entrepreneurs who love Jesus to start and grow their businesses. And in 2019 we expanded again into a 15,000 square foot space with a café, theatre, classrooms, media room and event space, and at the same time, launched and built a tiny home community for people experiencing homelessness. In total, the ministry, and the businesses took a nonprofit, a foundation, and three businesses to support the effort. It was an incredible amount of work but, we experienced incredible success. Along the way though, I increasingly noticed and recognized many of the patterns of behavior that were similar to what I had experienced in the prior two decades in business and volunteer ministry in my own church, of being left out of meetings, having my opinion minimized, my voice silenced, and having the men insist on taking over as soon as I had the effort up and running, labeling it their own, despite me being the founder and the leader. And though I was happy for a season to allow those behaviors in the interest of unity, it became more and more difficult the larger the project, but it also became clearer that sacrificing for the sake of unity was not mutual.

Though I and my team of both men and women were able to accomplish some incredible ministry from 2005 to 2021 I had a hard time grasping some of the things I experienced. Ultimately, I recognized that many of the pastors and even some of the other church leaders saw me as their administrator as opposed to a peer, and because I had already experienced this in the business world, I knew this wasn't something I would do well with moving forward. So, in September 2016, after a decade of serving in both volunteer and nonprofit ministry, I was becoming increasingly unsettled in the ministry environment, and I had my sights on returning to the entrepreneurial world where I felt much more comfortable, gifted, and anointed to do the work. As I prayed for that move, I heard God say, "Get ready, things are going to transition," and I was excited for it! Though I had no idea then it would take another five years for me to make the transition out of ministry.

The following year, as I worked to separate myself from the non-profit ministry, I began to realize letting go was not going to be as easy as I thought. I loved serving in the community and seeing people meet Jesus and get set free. I just didn't love the limiting environment and systems I had to work in. But that unsettled feeling, had now turned into a full blown "holy irritation" and I became laser focused on how some leaders in the church treated women. And while I knew that the holy irritation was one of the ways' God speaks to me when he's going to involve me in helping to change things, and that change usually comes through awareness, exposure, and correction; I also knew it usually meant that I would need to change too.

Meanwhile, I found myself questioning my own pastor about the injustices I experienced in ministry and the church's larger injustices toward women. His response to those questions, confirmed that he not only believed women could not be pastors, but that he also did not see biblical evidence of women leading in culture either. It was the first time he had ever said the part about women in leading in culture out loud, and I was confused in the moment, thinking I had somehow not paid enough attention or gotten it wrong somewhere along the way. Fifteen years prior when our family joined that church, we had resolved ourselves that we could accept the limitation that women could not be pastors, reasoning God had not called us or anyone in our circle to be a pastor. But I had never heard, understood, or accepted, that the limiting belief system also included women not leading in culture. Following that conversation, a lot of the behaviors I had experienced in the nonprofit ministry, and even my prior time in the corporate world, began to make much more sense. But then, he ended our conversation suggesting that I not dwell on it since it was not a "major" anyway. I knew that what that meant was that the Bible wasn't clear on its interpretation, and it did not affect someone's salvation.

That moment caused me to ask God what He really thought about women in leadership and question why He designed me the way He did, if He didn't want me to use the gifts. But it also caused me to question why the church was so immersed in stopping women from leading if the Bible wasn't clear on it. And it caused me to ask more questions and do more research on the church and it's limits on women, realizing I had accepted the teaching without ever researching it for myself. What I now understand is that what I believed was confusion on my part over the exact details of the limiting belief system around women, was actually an expansion of the belief system that took place gradually over time following the women's movement of the 1960's to today, more so in the more conservative denominations, including the ones I and my family attended, but almost every denomination has some form of them. Additionally, I also now understand that because of this belief system, women are often excluded from any type of discipleship process in many of these more traditional churches, leaving the women to discover much of the Bible on our own, outside of Sunday sermons and women's bible studies.

As a result, many women I know, have never researched the Bible for themselves outside of the church and have limited understanding of what God says about His design for women or that there is a roadmap for them in His Scripture that can guide them into developing a healthy identity, purpose, leadership and calling. That process of discipleship is intended to be extended to all believers, but in my journey and maybe yours too, it was minimized because of the limiting beliefs that women can even be called by God. That process is designed to equip you and I with spiritual maturity and bring peace and freedom to us as we become aligned with God. But when this important kingdom process is disrupted, that disruption produces hopelessness and a feeling of being rejected by God. This is where I found myself that day in the shower. To further complicate my confusion and exhaustion that day, I couldn't help but see the similarities in behavior that I experienced in the church, to what I experienced in my corporate career, and it left me wondering if I could ever escape the belief system that had kept me in bondage most of my life.

In my first career job, when I became pregnant with our first child, my boss demanded I be fired for having the edacity to do so! Following the conversation where he made that demand, I penned a letter to the company's owner citing the new discrimination laws, and he and I agreed that I would work until I was ready to go on maternity leave but that I was not welcome back after that. Three months following my daughter's birth, a female supervisor who helped me maneuver how to best tell the boss about my pregnancy, woke up after a company meeting with drugs in her system and evidence of a sexual encounter, effectually ending her career. These types of targeted attacks against women were not unusual for a woman who dared to work in a man's world in the early 1990's.

In my next job, despite intentionally seeking out and surrounding myself with women, including a female boss, after two years of experiencing incredible success and three promotions, an all-male leadership team was brought in, and about as quickly as the promotions came, they were taken away. Several months into my last promotion, on a visit from my new boss, he suggested we meet for dinner, where he confessed his love for me. I emphatically reminded him that we were both married with children and that nothing would come of his feelings. On the way home that night, he attempted to rape me. The next morning he confessed in writing to Human Resources and resigned his position in the company, but it didn't matter. Over the next four months I received threats and retaliation from the "good old boys" in leadership above him, who quickly "reorganized" my division and laid me off from my position in the company. The year was 2001.

During my corporate season, I didn't just experience the *big things,* I also worked in an environment that included a daily dose of behaviors limiting my ability to be and lead in a way that was consistent with my God given identity and purpose. Over the years, I was counseled to lose weight, dress more conservative and even more trendy including being bought clothes by my bosses; and I was trained to lead like the men. And I was o.k. with it at the time believing that the training would result in me getting to the top of the corporate ladder and experience the success of the top positions. But it didn't. In fact, I now understand that the behaviors, that were known and discussed amongst the men, were designed to do exactly the opposite and insure that I and other women did not reach those positions and earn those titles.

These circumstances, occurring early on in my career, have shaped so many other choices in my life as well as impacted who I am today. I had to choose to overcome them or remain bitter and mad, so I chose over and over again to overcome. But having to overcome often meant walking away from things I loved and disrupting what God meant for my good. Eventually, after working in a variety of other companies for a total of sixteen years in that industry, and never regaining my footing, I discovered how to build a business myself and have enjoyed starting and building companies since that time. Entrepreneurship is a great alternative, especially for women who love to lead but aren't necessarily given the chance to with the same kind of freedom afforded the men. And I have owned my own businesses since 2005. But re-engaging in ministry and seeing these similar behaviors in the church, especially years later when I assumed more strides had been made to welcome women in leadership, left me curious if the behaviors were somehow connected.

God has since reconciled the truth about many of the things that have happened over the years in both business and ministry, highlighting and connecting the patterns of behavior to the issue of women in leadership in both the Church and our culture as a whole, which I will also do for you as you read future chapters. But one of the reasons it was hard for me to discern what was happening with the belief system in these groups, is because no church that I encountered posted the belief system for others to see. Regardless, the behaviors were almost the same as the corporate world, a bit less aggressive but more broadly accepted and outwardly normalized, definitely wrapped in scripture, and virtually no one in leadership was questioning them. The conversations and many times the decision to develop their own plans, always took place behind closed doors. And the women were not only unaware these meetings were taking place, but the plans were also never shared with us afterwards. Being shut down in conversations, expecting us to do the work with no pay and taking credit for it, and labeling our work as theirs was the norm. And honestly, it became hard to not take it personally.

But some of the men who were in those rooms making those decisions began to speak the truth, sharing with me that many denominations and boards, have coached the men, especially pastors, not to get into discussions with women behind closed doors in general, but also not to stir up controversy by discussing the limiting beliefs. This explanation made sense to me, considering the reactions I would get when I asked questions, similar to the secrecy that I experienced in the business world and often kept within human resource departments, except that often when women did ask questions they were charged with stirring division and labeled "Jezebel". But I and other women I knew just wanted to understand why the behaviors still existed, what roadmap we should follow, and why they were being extended to settings in culture. But after repeated incidents and even experiencing women leaving churches, their ministries and even God, many of us grew weary of the behaviors and began to talk about what we could do to bring change.

God knew that we would not accept that the behaviors were intentional, as opposed to being by chance, unless we had tried everything to resolve the issues honorably, and there was evidence beyond any doubt that we could point to. But as I began to discreetly seek guidance from multiple leaders, both male and female, there were two divided responses around the behaviors. The first response, which came mostly from women but a few men, categorized the behavior as "abusive and not okay" and confirmed they had also seen and experienced many of these same limiting behaviors. I was not surprised by this of course because women have been talking amongst each other about it for a long time. But the second response, from both men and women was, "This is what it looks like to partner with the churches." The justification being that this behavior is prescribed and acceptable. I found myself unsettled by both answers.

I now understand that many of the same scenarios I experienced are familiar patterns that have been inflicted on many women leaders and that the pattern of behavior is absolutely, emphatically not of God. It's not endorsed by God, by Scripture, or by any human being that has any ounce of compassion or grace or truth of God. It is many times abusive. It is often harassment. It is most of the time discrimination, in the same way we recognize it as such in business. And worst, many of the behaviors are sin. But somehow, while culture is dealing with the issue in an ethical and compassionate way, it has become corporately accepted and is now part of social construct in the church. And many leaders, including myself at one time, are wrapping the behaviors in Scripture and calling it okay. And it's not okay.

So when God said, "Put the book about unity down, you have to address this first," I was in no position at the time and really had no experience in how to restore women to the Church, address the belief system, or what I believed that would entail, except that I had been a part of the changes in culture. What I felt in my spirit, though, was that I had obeyed all the rules. I had sat at the tables in silence. I had dressed down the way they wanted me to dress. I had allowed the men to take first position while I took second, even though I knew I was gifted, anointed, and often called, to take first. I had shut down most of my visions and dreams and learned to shut down my opinions and do things their way. And I had spent my entire life striving to be the perfect woman in the eyes of the Church, despite the inner toil it caused, and it did not make me a better believer, bring me peace, or result in God's desired outcomes for my life, for others' lives, or those of the church. And it definitely doesn't represent the heart of God. I believed God was asking me to do something about it, but I didn't know what and I didn't at the time even believe that I could change anything. But I knew God had a plan and I wanted to be a part of it.

Reflection

1. Sometimes God has us on a redemptive journey and we don't recognize until later that we are in a season that has a common theme. What seasons and common themes can you identify in your own journey?
2. How have those themes influenced your decisions?
3. Have you ever spent time in prayer asking God to let you see what He sees regarding your life or the frustrations you have in life?
4. What beliefs about women's roles do you have and where did you learn them?
5. Have you allowed some of those belief systems to limit you in your journey?

CHAPTER 2

THE POWER OF HER TRUTH

*"Then you will know the truth, and
the truth will set you free."*

—JOHN 8:32

The power of your truth is to become grounded enough in who you are and what you believe that you are immovable but not inflexible, to change the things you can and accept the things you can't. There is not enough paper and time to tell all of the disparaging stories and describe to you the depth of betrayal, that happened during my ministry season. At the same time, there are many stories of redemption and restoration that I can and will share with you as we progress. At the point that I finally closed the nonprofit ministry in 2021, because of the behaviors, I had a crisis of faith. I was pretty sure I could never trust the church and I wasn't sure I could trust God. And I know that many of you feel the same. The good news is that after going through this process, I don't feel that way now. Now

I know that I know that I know that God is real, that He loves me and I'm not only a part of His plan, but that He designed me exactly the way I am, and we *are* the Church! The first step to restore God's blueprint for your life is to replace all of the lies that you have believed and replace them with His Truth and allow Him to refine you along the way into the person He designed you to be.

We all have a combination of experiences and teaching that makes up our own truth and belief system. I used to believe that the way pastors, churches and denominations taught the Bible was the same. But I now know that is not true. One pastor friend of mine once said, "The truth of the Bible is as relevant as your experiences." What he meant by this is that your experiences cause you to dig deeper into the Bible to find God's answers to your situation. While I knew that the cause of women's roles being limited in culture likely originated in the Church, I needed to research it and understand it for myself. Despite graduating from college with a political science degree and being involved in women's issues politically and socially in many of my endeavors, I had never considered looking to politics to explain the Church' belief system. I had just accepted it wholeheartedly.

As I asked God to reveal to me how to reconcile everything that I had experienced and believed, He asked me to consider the influences in my life and research those influences. I eventually recognized four influences that diminished the power of my truth. The first influence came from being raised in Southern Baptist churches that I know were spirit filled and freedom focused when I was young but are now one of the denominations pushing the traditional view of women and the limiting belief system around women's roles in leadership. The second influence was politics and political agendas that I now know were used to extend the limiting beliefs of the church to culture, designed to limit my leadership even in the business world. And the third and fourth were topics we didn't discuss much in the denomination I was raised in: how to have an active relationship with the Holy Spirit coupled with the authority to defend myself from the strategies of Satan and spiritual warfare and how those strategies played into some of my experiences.

I was raised in white, evangelical, mostly Southern Baptist churches in the Bible Belt, namely the midwestern portion of the United States. We were taught to respect authority, work hard, and submit to our elders. When I was younger, I experienced the excitement and hope of Jesus and revival in these churches, but by the time I reached high school, churches were splitting over the tiniest differences. My grandmother had dreams and visions and led the family spiritually, and then my dad assumed that role after she passed. One area of confusion for me was that I knew that my grandmother had taught and even preached in the church, but as I got older, I was taught that this wasn't allowed. I didn't understand until doing the research for this book that this was a shift in belief in the Southern Baptist Convention. When I would ask my dad about it, he would say, "I don't know where these churches get the idea that women can't preach or lead in the church. That's not what the Bible says." At the same time, he definitely expected my mom to stay in the home while he went to work which I now know was one of the ways Scripture was used in partnership with politics to limit women. I was also raised to believe that pastors deserve honor and trust and that they were responsible for my spiritual growth as I submitted to their leadership. For the most part, I still believe in these principles, though in a much healthier way grounded in Scripture.

What I discovered in ministry as an adult, though, is that all churches and all pastors are different and that none are perfect. Those differences are often similar to the reasons you and I are different: we came from different cultures, were raised in different environments, have different strengths, and were taught by different seminaries or denominations which carry great authority over what pastors are taught. While I still trust many pastors immensely and believe that most pastors and leaders in the Church agree on the foundations of the Bible, the men themselves are not the inerrant Word of God; only

Jesus is. This realization led me to understand that I had trusted pastors alone to teach me the Bible, instead of researching it for myself. In doing so, I had unintentionally removed much of the power of God in my life. Today, after going through my own personal spiritual bootcamp with Jesus and the Holy Spirit, I now read the Bible with much more intention and rigor, paying attention to the meaning contextually, spiritually, and culturally. If you have never read the Bible in this way and have always relied on others' interpretations, including those found in books and Bible studies, to tell you what it says, you may want to revisit that approach.

As I became more aware of the differences among churches and pastors, I observed that those differences were often consistent with their respective giftings and that their preaching and leadership styles reflected this. The operating system that God gifted each of them with—apostolic, prophetic, evangelistic, pastoral, or teacher—was not only the lens that they taught through, but it was also the factor that attracted certain people to their churches. For example, apostolic leaders are often more focused on church planting and building, pastors on caring for the congregation and teachers on teaching the bible. Additionally, when you add the geography, culture, life experiences, upbringing, and other environmental factors, each church is as different as each individual is. Different churches have different expressions of the truth, distinctions that God has placed in them, and I am blessed to have visited and experienced many different churches over the years. But there were still a few of them I had not been to and had even avoided because of my belief system namely the charismatic churches. So as God began to heal me with His truth, He also began to orchestrate encounters designed perfectly for what I needed to hear and that would allow me to experience all of Him, in all of his expressions.

The first time I heard a gospel message that included women being able to preach was in late 2015 at a pastors conference, at fifty years old after being saved at age seven! The speakers that day began to outline Scriptures interpreted in a much different way than I had ever heard them, mainly emphasizing that much of the Scripture around women is inconclusive and can be interpreted in a few ways, leaving the decision up to the church leadership. As they completed their presentation and provided some resources for people to read later, I felt a little excited at the possibility that these interpretations could be true, but I wasn't quite ready to give up my belief system of forty years after one conference! Regardless, that day became the beginning of a journey to understand the truth about how God designed and commissioned women, including leaders in top positions, and how Jesus advocated for them during His ministry. I did read all of the books they recommended (see the Resource section at the back of this book), while God personally took me on a deep dive into the scriptures involving women in the Bible.

In 2017, around the same time that God started transitioning me out of the nonprofit ministry, and my restlessness turned into a holy irritation, I also began to desire to know more about the Holy Spirit. In 2018 I attended another conference where I was reintroduced to the Holy Spirit and the spiritual gifts, including the five leadership functions I referenced earlier, also referred to as the fivefold ministry. With this new understanding, I learned how to see, hear, know, and experience God better and more actively. In the more conservative churches I had previously attended, though the Holy Spirit was present, He was more of a helper to convict believers of their sin. Similarly, the spiritual gifts were taught but they were more of a litmus test for believers to strive to attain rather than something "gifted" to you by the Holy Spirit. We did not prophesy and the fivefold functions— apostle, prophet, evangelist, pastor, teacher—were never mentioned. But when I heard them described for the first time at this conference, I immediately understood so much more about how God designed me and why I think and do things certain ways. Somehow, they really made sense to me right away. Maybe because they seemingly lined up in a similar way to roles and titles I was accustomed to and understood in business: the founder (apostle), the builder (prophet), the salesperson (evangelist), human resources (pastor), and operations (teacher).

Again, I left the conference with books and a desire to understand more. The next year, in 2019, after studying, reading, and researching more about these spiritual gifts, I returned to the same conference, this time though the Holy Spirit and I were speaking regularly, and He had me focused intently on learning more again about women in leadership in the church. A young woman was introduced and came to the stage to speak to us that day, her exact message I don't even remember! I just know that as I sat there listening, I cried tears of sorrow at the sound of her voice. I now understood better how to talk to God, so I asked the Holy Spirit why I was so sad and what it was that I was hearing. He said, "You just heard the *feminine voice of God*, and your sadness is because you are mourning that you've never heard it before." I was wrecked after that and began sobbing uncontrollably, with a deep sense of grief. This woman, designed in God's image and operating authentically and fully in it, was speaking in a voice and language I could understand. I knew at that moment that God had not designed women to be second or sit on the sidelines. And I knew that I could no longer sit under a leader or church who taught otherwise.

The second influence in my life around the issue of women in leadership was how the church used politics to extend the limited beliefs to culture. During this same season starting in 2017, the #metoo, #churchtoo, and renewed racial reconciliation movements began to gain momentum, and I became aware of two terms I had never heard before: complementarianism and egalitarianism. Complementarianism holds that men and women have different but complementary roles and responsibilities in the family and in the church, though many have now extended it to life and culture as well. Egalitarianism maintains that those roles and responsibilities should remain equally available to men and women. The term complementarianism was not coined until 1988 by the founders of the Council of Biblical Manhood and Womanhood (CBMW). According to their website, CBMW. org, "The Danvers Statement summarizes the need for the Council on Biblical Manhood and Womanhood (CBMW) and serves as an overview of our core beliefs. This statement was prepared by several evangelical leaders at a CBMW meeting in Danvers, Massachusetts, in December of 1987. It was first published in final form by the CBMW in Wheaton, Illinois in November of 1988."[1]

Additionally, the CBMW founders acknowledged that the reason for the statement was in response to "biblical feminism" and that their mission was to "equip the church on the meaning of biblical sexuality." Their website also acknowledges that in 1998, the Southern Baptist Convention (SBC), the largest Protestant denomination in the United States, followed suit and adopted the Danvers Statement and complementarianism as part of their statement of faith. That acknowledgement on the CBMW website that the SBC had adopted the Danvers statement, led me to the SBC's website where I discovered that on June 1, 1984, a few years prior to the Danvers Statement, "The Resolution on Ordination and the Role of Women in Ministry" was passed by the SBC, stating, "Therefore, be it RESOLVED, That we not decide concerns of Christian doctrine and practice by modern cultural, sociological, and ecclesiastical trends or by emotional factors; that we remind ourselves of the dearly bought Baptist principle of the final authority of Scripture in matters of faith and conduct; and that we encourage the service of women in all aspects of church life and work other than pastoral functions and leadership roles entailing ordination."[2]

This was the first time I had ever connected the dots and seen in writing that prior to these proclamations women had been ordained as pastors. I was finally able to reconcile completely the confusion between my childhood understanding and my adult experience, recognizing that while the denomination had at one time ordained women as pastors, it no longer did. This is the same denomination in which I was baptized in 1972 and followed later in life. It is also the same denomination of many pastors and churches I know well, of the theological seminaries these pastors attended, and of Lifeway Christian Resources, the publisher of most of the books, Bible studies, and resources I read and studied over the years. Additionally, during the editing process for this book, the SBC took a further stand on this topic and now is moving to remove women from all leadership positions in the denomination.

In February 2023, Pastor Rick Warren of Saddleback church made news as he took a stand against complementarianism, ordaining women as pastors in his own church, and was subsequently kicked out of the denomination after 88 percent of the denomination's delegates affirmed the decision against ordaining women. On February 21, the Southern Baptist Convention's executive committee voted to expel Saddleback church and five other churches for ordaining women. In Pastor Warren's subsequent apology to women posted to Twitter on June 10, 2023[3], included in the final chapter of this book, he admits regretfully buying into the belief of the denomination without ever researching the issue for himself. After thousands of years of the Bible's existence, in a secret meeting of men only, a new term was coined to limit the roles of women and to extend those restrictions to all areas of culture through four main scriptures in the Bible:

1. "Women should remain silent in the churches" (1 Corinthians 14:34–35).

2. "But I do not allow a woman to teach or exercise authority over a man, but to remain quiet" (1 Timothy 2: 11–15).

3. "Wives, submit to your own husbands, as to the Lord. For the husband is the head of the wife even as Christ is the head of the church, his body, and is himself its Savior. Now as the church submits to Christ, so also wives should submit in everything to their husbands" (Ephesians 5:22–24).

4. "It is not good that the man should be alone; I will make him a helper as his partner" (Genesis 2:18).

The amount of time between when I first heard a gospel message supporting women in leadership to when I finally changed my mind about the limiting beliefs that I'd previously adopted in my life as truth was three years. It took that long—mostly because of my inability to hear it. It would be another four years before I heard any other man in pastoral leadership affirm the belief, mostly because doing so has consequences. If you are a layman and embrace this truth about women leaders according to the Bible, you have everything to gain. But if you are a pastor, or church leader, or a denomination leader, and you embrace this, you have something to lose. I have seen and know pastors who do the research and change their minds about women's roles in churches: they don't just lose friendships with other pastors; they lose many in their congregations who have heard the limited teaching for so long and, like me, see it as heretical. And though many in the Church genuinely believe that Scripture denies certain positions to women in the church, when asked if they can defend their position Scripturally, they cannot because they are either completely oblivious to the continued narrowing of Scripture or have never researched it for themselves.

As God began to open my eyes to these truths, I started speaking up to others who were in many of the circles that I had found myself in during ministry. What I found is that very few people I knew actually believed in the doctrine of complementarianism and most did not even know what the term meant, yet they accepted and even participated in the limiting behaviors. You will not find the term complementarianism or the acceptance of it posted on most church websites. The secrecy around the meetings that coined the term and its insertion into the political agenda in America, calling it "traditional family values," has been so mainstream that many people who are passionate about Jesus don't even understand the connection or what they are really agreeing with. Further, the Church has become a place for friendships, building community, and status, so many people are afraid to take a stand for Jesus and the Bible for fear of losing what they have at church. For me and my husband, despite not agreeing with those limiting beliefs personally, we continued to go to churches that subscribed to them, thinking it didn't matter to us or to our children. But that was far from the truth. Your decision to remain in these belief systems, especially if you're not committed to the belief, will have a lasting impact on your personal identity, purpose, leadership and calling, as well as that of your family, and your family legacy, in a similar way that it did in culture, except in the church the consequences are eternal.

The pandemic became an accelerant for many people in the Church, including me, to be able to experience the same diversity of preaching that it took me years to find. Social media and the need for churches to reach congregants in their homes instead of a building made it much easier to hear various expressions of the truth instead of being limited to the truth of one preacher. The Church had to transition to meet the times. But the transition is not over. The Church now finds itself in a position of being fact-checked by people who may or may not believe in Jesus and the Bible, and now have a greater ability to cross-check different pastors and churches. So whether we like it or not, this issue and others will be at the forefront of future debate, and as believers we will have to press into the details and be able to defend the Bible, corporately or individually, or lose all credibility.

And while the discovery of the change in the belief system in the Southern Baptist Convention and the Danvers Statement helped me reconcile my own memories of my grandmother preaching and lead-ing churches when I was young, it opened up some new questions in me. I had always been taught that pastors received a special calling and anointing from God that only men could receive and that it was how God used men specifically to protect the inerrant word of God. If that was the case, then why does it need to be a secret? And why do the meetings take place in secret? And why were women allowed to lead and preach in the more conservative churches I was raised prior to the early 1980's and then it changed? If it was the inerrant Word of God, how did they get the memo that God wanted to change it? The secrecy of the meetings and the partnership with politics to seemingly control women in culture following the women's movements, while openly admitting it was a reaction to *biblical feminism*, was something I couldn't find peace around. In Luke 12:1-3 Jesus is speaking to a crowd and says this, "Be on your guard against the yeast of the Pharisees, which is hypocrisy. There is nothing concealed that will not be disclosed or hidden that will not be made known. What you have said in the dark will be heard in the daylight, and what you have whispered in the ear in the inner rooms will be proclaimed from the roofs."

During each phase of this journey, I didn't even know I was on a journey that had purpose. I was just trying to live my life and live it in a way that was honorable and focused on God. But I now know that as God began to reveal the truth to me, He had to give each portion of it to me at the right time and in the right way so that I could receive it. First, I had to hear the truth about some of my experiences. Then God exposed and corrected the truth about women in leadership, but I also had to live it, try it out, and research it for myself. Then He reintroduced the Holy Spirit and spiritual gifts to me, and I got to spend some time with the Holy Spirit on my own so I could really understand and get to know how the Spirit works. And once I understood that relationship, then I was in position to hear the feminine voice of God. God could have given me all of these things at once, but He didn't. Though we will spend much more time in future chapters talking about the Holy Spirit and all of the wonderful things He guides us through, the first step was to have God walk us through His Word start the process of building us back up to be the person He designed and purposes us to be.

Reflection

1. Where does your truth come from, people or the Bible itself? How do you know this?
2. How do you test if what others are telling you is true biblical interpretation?
3. Have you ever heard the feminine voice of God? Describe your experience.
4. Have you ever considered how the term pastor now encompasses all types of gifting? Elaborate.
5. How can differences among churches be consistent with God's plan?

CHAPTER 3

THE POWER OF
HER DESIGN

"Out of my distress I called on the LORD;
the Lord answered me and set me free."

—PSALM 118:5 (ESV)

The power of your design is knowing He is for you and standing with you regardless of what any man says or does. As awful as the journey and discovering the truth was for me, it caused me to get to know God, Jesus, and the Holy Spirit in ways I never had. I had a very skewed view of the three expressions of God we call the Trinity and many other theological truths that God had to correct. So by 2020 when the pandemic hit, I not only needed rest, but I needed to soak up God's love and His promises with tears and laughter as I processed my journey in the church. But I also desperately needed to find women referenced in the Word and see how we have always been part of God's plan. I now knew what the Holy Spirit had told me and what truth was now in me. And I also knew that at least some of the

Church had made some changes to their belief system that negated many of the beliefs I had been taught. But what really mattered most to me, was what Jesus thought. I pray that this chapter blesses you in the same way this stage of the journey blessed me as God walked me through it. It's time to start building you back up. There is a warrior within you, and there are legions of angels surrounding you and your destiny. Jesus is walking right next to you, while the Holy Spirit guides your understanding and God moves mountains and commands evil to stand down to protect you and to see that you walk in freedom.

God had met me in the shower to announce the name of this book, as I've mentioned, and I responded to it with giggling and tears knowing it meant He was for us. However, I nevertheless struggled afterward to understand what it would mean to you the reader. Why *Jesus in Pink*? For some, the color pink invokes good memories and for others, not so good. I've talked to women who were raised with so much pink they never wore it again, while others like me who never resonated with the color pink, are soaking it up now, making up for lost time. There are a few reasons I think God wanted the title to be *Jesus in Pink*, the first being that He knew there would be an attack on feminine identity at the time this book was being released. The second is what I expressed in the introduction, that you and I need to know that Jesus is for us and is standing with us in this fight; He did not die for us and then ask us to be less than what He designed us to be. The third reason is that the color pink in culture today represents the full spectrum of girls, women, and our causes, ranging from soft pink to hot pink. And the fourth reason, the biblical interpretation of the color pink is "new life." It actually represents what Jesus did for us on the cross. I knew I needed to revisit everything that I believed with a new lens, perhaps a pink one. The first thing I did was ask Jesus to walk with me through His Word and help me see myself and other women in it, and I asked Him to give me His Word three different ways so I would know whatever I was hearing and learning was from Him.

For me, usually the first way He would alert me to something was through a dream or a vision. Sometimes it would be as I was going about my day, but often it was in the middle of the night. And He would direct me to a word or a topic and have me research it in the Bible. There were days when I would spend a full day or days winding through a topic so He could show me things I had never noticed. And then, as He promised, He would have a friend call out of the blue to confirm what I had just read, or a stranger give me a prophetic word, or a song on the radio speak to the topic. And finally, He would bring me a written resource as final confirmation. What I now know is that He was teaching me many foundational truths that build on each other and make up His blueprint that we find in His Word about women.

Next, He sat with me as I worked through the scriptures that had been and are still being used as weapons against women. He highlighted what He wanted me to see and research further and showed me the context of those scriptures. For example, in 1 Corinthians 14:34–35, the scripture that is used to say women should remain silent, Paul was specifically addressing a certain group of women in a certain church, and this was not meant to be a universal prescription for the Church; it also contradicts other things Paul said in other parts of the Bible. In 1 Timothy 2:11–15, which is used to justify women not exercising authority over a man because of her indiscretion in the garden, Paul is in fact again instructing a particular church in a particular city where women were "domineering" the meetings. Ephesians 5:22–24 is used to say wives need to submit to their husbands, but it also says husbands need to submit to their wives, so Paul was likely asking men, as the more prominent partner in the marriage relationship at the time, to treat their wives like Christ would. Finally, Genesis 2:18 is used to argue that women were designed as man's "helper," but the meaning of the original word here actually denotes a co-heir—in other words, men and women functioning together as the combined image of God. Though I'm sharing these as the ones highlighted to me in my journey, they are not an exhaustive list of scriptures used to limit women, nor are they the complete explanation of men's and women's roles according to Scripture. That is a much longer discussion many authors spend an entire book covering. But you can check the resources in the back for more information and further research to allow yourself to dive deeper into these scriptures.

After God addressed these scriptures with me, He started taking me through more and more Scripture using the pink lens. First and foremost, we are all made in God's image. Genesis 1:27 says, "So God created mankind in his own image, in the image of God he created him; male and female he created them." Genesis 1:28 says, "God blessed them and said to them, 'Be fruitful and increase in number; fill the earth and subdue it. Rule over the fish in the sea and the birds in the sky and over every living creature that moves on the ground." And finally, Genesis 2:22–24 says, "Then the LORD God made a woman from the rib he had taken out of the man, and he brought her to the man. The man said, 'This is now bone of my bones and flesh of my flesh; she shall be called "woman," for she was taken out of man.' That is why a man leaves his father and mother and is united to his wife, and they become one flesh." As I read these words, they landed in my spirit like never before. First, I didn't remember ever reading the words that way, and second, it had never been taught to me that way. I was always taught that creation started in the garden with Adam and Eve and that Eve caused all men and women to be cursed. But when I first read Genesis 1:27 God put the emphasis on us, both male and female, being created in God's image and He highlighted the word *him* interpreted as "mankind," used to include both male and female. Then in Genesis 1:28 "He gives us authority over everything on the earth and asks us to care for it." Next, God highlighted woman coming out of man and that when they marry, they become one again. This has to mean that God created us together but then separated us so that each of us would carry part of His image, and those parts complement each other. Nowhere in these verses does the Bible discuss titles or positions! Also I noticed the word *him* in Genesis meaning *mankind*, would indicate that there is distinction at minimum in the beginning that God did not intend for every *him* in the Bible to mean man.

God then took me to the scriptures that talk about God's image being referenced in the feminine. I should note here that this exercise of splitting the Bible into parts that apply to men versus women was never God's intent, and it is impossible to split the scripture between male and female, without negating much of it for women, or men for that matter. Ultimately trying to do so becomes the best argument anyone could give that the entire Bible was intended for all believers, male and female, as the splitting would wipe out much of the new covenant for women. But still, God wanted me to see that He is also described in feminine terms in the Bible. In Deuteronomy 32:11, God is like a mother eagle hovering over her young. Hosea 13:8 tells us that God experiences the fury of a mother bear robbed of her cubs. In Isaiah 49:15 He is like a woman who would never forget her nursing child. God will not forget His children. In Isaiah 66:13 we're told God comforts His people like a mother comforts her child. In Luke 13:34 Jesus longed for the people of Jerusalem, like a mother hen longing to gather her chicks under her wings. In Luke 15:8–10, we're shown that God seeks the lost like a housekeeper trying to find her lost coins. And according to Psalm 22:9–10 and 71:6 and also Isaiah 66:9, God cares for His people like a midwife who cares for the child she just delivered.

As you read through these scriptures, try not to let your belief system dictate their meaning. For example, I have heard these scriptures taught in a way that highlighted the positional component of the scriptures that focuses on the title or hierarchical position of the leader versus the relational behavior that focuses on the attributes of the behavior. If you were looking at it from a positional perspective, you would see mother, nursing child, mother hen, housekeeper, and midwife. But if you were looking at it from a relational standpoint as many women do, you might notice different things. For example, the feminine image of God hovering or having fury denotes He is a protector, and never forgetting His children denotes His love and His faithfulness. In His feminine image, He comforts His children and gathers them under His wing, emphasis on *comforting* and *gathering*. Then He searches for them, never giving up on them. And finally, in His feminine image, He cares for His children. Interestingly, these two lenses—positional and relational—will take on greater significance as we move forward in the identity restoration journey. We will see their correlation, as statistics show, between men's and women's strengths, respectively.

Next God wanted me to see how intentional He was about creating me and you. Take, for example, Psalms 139:13 where David is praising God and says, "For you created my inmost being; you knit me together in my mother's womb." Now consider Proverbs 31 where David's mother tells him what to look for in a wife, not because they are a curse but because they are a blessing! Nowhere in the context of Proverbs 31 is it suggested that the chapter is a prescription for what women can or cannot do or be. Yet it has been used so many times to justify the argument that women's place is in the home. For fun, try reading these attributes listed in Proverbs 31 through the two different lenses, positional versus relational.

- She possesses strength and valor.
- She is full of wealth and wisdom.
- She brings victory.
- She brings good.
- She seeks out things that are pure and righteous.
- She likes to work.
- She gives out revelation.
- She spiritually nourishes others.
- She labors to plant living vines.
- She sets her heart on fields and takes them as her own.

- She wraps herself in strength, might, and power in all of her works.
- She is light in darkness.
- She is not afraid of tribulation.
- She covers her household in dual garments of righteousness and grace.
- Her clothing is beautiful and made from exquisite materials.
- She loves her enemies.
- She exudes power, majesty, laughter, and joy.
- She teaches wisdom and kindness.
- She has loving instruction from her lips.
- She watches over her household and needs.
- Her family extols her.
- She lives in wonder, awe, and fear of the Lord.
- She will be praised.
- Others should give her the credit she is due.
- Her loving works should be admired at the gateways of every city.

After Proverbs 31, God reminded me of how He feels about us and what He wants for us, and that love is the greatest commandment of all. In Galatians 5:13–14 we're reminded that Paul says, "You, my brothers, and sisters, were called to be free. But do not use your freedom to indulge the flesh; rather, serve one another humbly in love. For the entire law is fulfilled in keeping this one command: 'Love your neighbor as yourself.'"

In 1 Corinthians 13:4–8, we are reminded, "Love is patient, love is kind. It does not envy, it does not boast, it is not proud. It does not dishonor others, it is not self-seeking, it is not easily angered, it keeps no record of wrongs. Love does not delight in evil but rejoices with the truth. It always protects, always trusts, always hopes, always perseveres. Love never fails." Jesus came to bring freedom to us, all of us, from the curse of the law and the garden and to bring new life with the new covenant.

Romans 8:1–4 further says, "Therefore, there is now no condemnation for those who are in Christ Jesus, because through Christ Jesus the law of the Spirit who gives life has set you free from the law of sin and death. For what the law was powerless to do because it was weakened by the flesh, God did by sending his own Son in the likeness of sinful flesh to be a sin offering. And so he condemned sin in the flesh, in order that the righteous requirement of the law might be fully met in us, who do not live according to the flesh but according to the Spirit."

Finally, in John 8:1–11, we read that Jesus called out the Pharisees and defended the woman caught in adultery, when they wanted to hold a woman to the law:

Jesus went to the Mount of Olives.

At dawn he appeared again in the temple courts, where all the people gathered around him, and he sat down to teach them. The teachers of the law and the Pharisees brought in a woman caught in adultery. They made her stand before the group and said to Jesus, "Teacher, this woman was caught in the act of adultery. In the Law Moses commanded us to stone such women. Now what do you say?" They were using this question as a trap, in order to have a basis for accusing him.

But Jesus bent down and started to write on the ground with his finger. When they kept on questioning him, he straightened up and said to them, "Let any one of you who is without sin be the first to throw a stone at her." Again he stooped down and wrote on the ground.

At this, those who heard began to go away one at a time, the older ones first, until only Jesus was left, with the woman still standing there. Jesus straightened up and asked her, "Woman, where are they? Has no one condemned you?"

"No one, sir," she said.

"Then neither do I condemn you," Jesus declared. "Go now and leave your life of sin."

Lastly, God walked me through some amazing examples of women in the Bible. Again, God highlighted character traits, but He also confirmed that each of these leaders acted in obedience to Him and that many of them had positions and titles. As we look at leading ladies of the Bible, Deborah is a great example of a woman leader. Deborah confronted the powers of darkness with the power of God. She called herself a mother to Israel and held the office of judge. As a judge, she had influence over people and people trusted her. She judged, provided wisdom, and dispensed justice. And she did not apologize for her anointing and grace to lead as she called out false worship and idolatry. She exposed corruption and mediated disputes, and she protected Israel. And in the process of leading, she gained the trust of Barak who understood Deborah was called.[4] This is such an important distinction. Barak understood that she was called to lead and that he was called to come alongside her. I just want to stop here and break off the lie that Deborah was an afterthought, and that Barak did not fail. For most of my life, I only heard the version of this story suggesting that if men don't step up to lead, women will fill the void. This is a lie that you should not partner with! It is inconsistent with the redemptive message in the Bible, yet I, and many other women I have talked to have believed such lies for too long. Part of moving forward is to also read the Bible with a lens of restoration, for both men and women, which is how it was intended to be received.

Another great woman of the Bible, Esther, prayed to God for change and was obedient to the things God asked of her. And that obedience stopped the plans of the enemy and brought freedom to her people. She was also loyal to her people and sacrificed what was best for herself and chose what was good for the nation. But let's stop again and correct twisted scripture interpretation. What Esther had to endure was part of an old structure and an old way. It is the part of history that was redeemed when Christ was born and died for us! Being enslaved or being used for sexual exploitation is not God's desire or will for women. So let's break this lie. This is also not of Jesus.

Sarah and Mary, two other prominent women in the Bible, birthed physical children, but they also birthed nations! Priscilla was a tent-maker and an apostle. We also see in the Bible that woman carried attributes of birthing, not just babies, but businesses and churches and ministries that changed lives. Women were life givers and nurturers. They are described in their work as having wisdom, perseverance, faith, joy, and kindness while at the same time being fierce warriors, advocates, and bridge builders and stopping the enemy from his schemes. We also see women holding offices of royalty, governance, and leadership, and often being at the forefront of ushering in cultural and theological shifts during times of oppression and war.

The Bible is rich with women whose attributes are both good and bad, just like it is with men. Women operated in a world that gave them much less freedom than we have today, and they still rose to great levels of leadership and accomplishment, relative to their times. And they are also in the Bible! The point here is this. These women were obedient to God, not man. They sought Him out and did what He prompted them to do when it was time. And because of their obedience, they also had titles and held positions that had great power and influence that changed nations. There is not one attribute or position that a woman might carry that was left out of the potential for women. But the one commonality they shared and the reason they are in the Bible is because of their relationship with God!

There was one last question I wanted to research as God restored my view of my own womanhood relative to Scripture, and that is; are men and women different from each other? That question has been the subject of many books, including ones that many in churches use to separate us based on position or attributes. And while I know that there are ways that women do things that are different in the way men do them, many of the limiting beliefs are based around position and title, not attributes. Conversely, most of the leadership training I have received was around how to lead through attributes, emphasizing the positive attributes of leadership mostly through a male lens. In all of the preceding Scriptures, did you see differences in attributes? Did you see differences in position or what types of things women can or can't do regarding purpose or calling? Regarding the things we can or can't do, I found just one difference, women can give birth and have an innate ability to nurture that life from inception to birth and even through adulthood. But what about through attributes? Gallup Strengths, one of the best assessments around strengths one might use at work, reports, "In Gallup's database of more than 7 million people who have taken the Clifton StrengthsFinder, we have found that men and women have four of the same top five strengths: Learner, Responsibility, Achiever, and Relator. The two we don't have in common as an aggregate population are Strategic for men and Empathy for women. In addition, women tend to lead with Responsibility, while men lead with Achiever."[5] What can we conclude from this? We will explore this topic more as we move forward, but for now, every leadership position in the church and culture is represented in the Bible in some way through stories of both women and men. Having said that, how we do things is another story.

I hope that a recap of the journey to the truth, specifically highlighting women and God's promises and design through a pink lens, has been helpful. Knowing how God wired us and continues to walk with us is key to learning to walk in freedom, even when others don't believe we can. Start by making some of these truths a declaration that reminds you who He is. *His promises are true, and I can trust Him. He designed me in His image. I am blessed, not cursed. I was knitted together in my mother's womb. I am uniquely designed to incubate, nurture, and partner with God to create life, while at the same time not limited in my attributes, calling, or position. Women in the Bible held every position. Jesus's example was to love, have compassion for, protect, advocate for, and support women and their causes.*

The first steps of the journey to wholeness and healing were for God to restore the truth about the limiting belief system I had believed, how politics played a role and the promises His Scripture contains about women. I pray that as you read through these scriptures as many times as it takes for you to believe that God loves you as much as the men, that you too will be healed by the truth. The next step was for God to expand my perspective by helping me build a fuller relationship with the Holy Spirit.

Reflection

1. How have you been able to apply God's promises in your life?
2. Have you considered what it means to be designed in God's image and what part of His image is in you?
3. When you read these scriptures, do you see any references to God's design being title and position? If no, then what is His focus when describing women?
4. What parts of who you are have you had to shut down because of the opinions of others?
5. What parts of who you are have you had to shut down specifically because you are leading men.

CHAPTER 4

THE POWER OF HER SPIRIT

"But you will receive power when the Holy Spirit comes on you; and you will be my witnesses in Jerusalem, and in all Judea and Samaria, and to the ends of the earth."

—ACTS 1:8

The Power of your Spirit is the same power that all believers have as a result of a relationship with the Holy Spirit. The Holy Spirit is defined in the Scripture as "helper". According to Miriam Webster the meaning of the Holy Spirit is the "third person of the Christian Trinity". In John 14:16-17, Jesus says this about the Holy Spirit, "And I will ask the Father, and he will give you another advocate to help you and be with you forever— the Spirit of truth. The world cannot accept him because it neither sees him nor knows him. But you know him, for he lives with you and will be in you."

At this point of the journey, I was having a hard time not being angry if I'm being honest. I not only felt betrayed in the way that many of the church leaders had treated me during my season in ministry, but I also felt betrayed by the Church and the more conservative denominations I grew up in that had to have understood that the belief system was altered in the 1980's. And then to add to it my own agreement with the belief system and not listening to my gut that something was not right, really made me question how I could move forward. Another point of contention for me, outside of my own circumstances, was the way that many churches show up for a ministry event, only if it brings value to the appearance the church was doing good in the community, (their words not mine) and leave when the hard work became messy but necessary. We will explore this further in future chapters, but when I had to look into the eyes of twenty-six people who had previously experienced homelessness and tell them that the homes we had gifted and promised them would be their forever homes, sometimes with huge fanfare at large events, would no longer be the case, I was devastated. I had to question, why we were doing all of these things if there is no power in the ministry to keep our promises, and further, give people what they really needed in order to be set free. I needed to know the Holy Spirit better, so God started to paint a picture of the role of the Holy Spirit for me.

In Matthew 3:11, we see that John knew Jesus was going to do more than he could. "I baptize you with water for repentance. But after me comes one who is more powerful than I, whose sandals I am not worthy to carry. He will baptize you with the Holy Spirit and fire." In Acts 2:1-4, we can see that, When the day of Pentecost came, they were all together in one place. Suddenly a sound like the blowing of a violent wind came from heaven and filled the whole house where they were sitting. They saw what seemed to be tongues of fire that separated and came to rest on each of them. All of them were filled with the Holy Spirit and began to speak in other tongues as the Spirit enabled them."

In John 16:7-14 Jesus said this; "But very truly I tell you, it is for your good that I am going away. Unless I go away, the Advocate will not come to you; but if I go, I will send him to you. When he comes, he will prove the world to be in the wrong about sin and righteousness and judgment: about sin, because people do not believe in me; about righteousness, because I am going to the Father, where you can see me no longer; and about judgment, because the prince of this world now stands condemned. I have much more to say to you, more than you can now bear. But when he, the Spirit of truth, comes, he will guide you into all the truth. He will not speak on his own; he will speak only what he hears, and he will tell you what is yet to come. He will glorify me because it is from me that he will receive what he will make known to you."

In John 14:25-26 it says, "All this I have spoken while still with you. But the Advocate, the Holy Spirit, whom the Father will send in my name, will teach you all things and will remind you of everything I have said to you." I love that the word advocate is used in this translation. Each translation is a little different. I have used the NIV throughout this entire book for consistency but also it was the version we were encouraged to use in the churches I attended, and I wanted to illustrate that the truth is there, regardless of translation, if you want to see it. The Greek word "Parakletos" in this passage is translated "Helper" in the English Standard Version of the Bible, "Advocate" in the NIV, and "Counselor" in the King James Version. The meaning of this word relates to "legal counsel."[6]

In Acts 2:38, "Peter replied, "Repent and be baptized, every one of you, in the name of Jesus Christ for the forgiveness of your sins. And you will receive the gift of the Holy Spirit." In Romans 8:6 we see that, "The mind governed by the flesh is death, but the mind governed by the Spirit is life and peace." And in Romans 8:26-27 it says, In the same way, the Spirit helps us in our weakness. We do not know what we ought to pray for, but the Spirit himself intercedes for us through wordless groans. And he who searches our hearts knows the mind of the Spirit, because the Spirit intercedes for God's people in accordance with the will of God."

In Galatians 5:16-18 it says, So I say, walk by the Spirit, and you will not gratify the desires of the flesh. For the flesh desires what is contrary to the Spirit, and the Spirit what is contrary to the flesh. They are in conflict with each other, so that you are not to do whatever you want. But if you are led by the Spirit, you are not under the law." And in Galatians 5:22-25 we learn, "But the fruit of the Spirit is love, joy, peace, forbearance, kindness, goodness, faithfulness, gentleness, and self-control. Against such things there is no law. Those who belong to Christ Jesus have crucified the flesh with its passions and desires. Since we live by the Spirit, let us keep in step with the Spirit."

In 1 Thessalonians 5:19 it warns, "Do not quench the Spirit." And finally, in Romans 15:13, "May the God of hope fill you with all joy and peace as you trust in him, so that you may overflow with hope by the power of the Holy Spirit."

The Holy Spirit was prophesied. He came and fell on the disciples, and He helped them bring the power of Jesus to crowds even after Jesus left. Today, He helps us pray when we don't know what to say. He brings us hope and the fruit of the spirit comes when we are in relationship with the Holy Spirit. He is our teacher, advocate, and counselor. He intercedes on our behalf when we don't have the words, according to the will of God. And He is our helper when we are in need. This is obviously not an exhaustive list of the Holy Spirit. If you learned about the Holy Spirit the way I did, and you have not experienced the fullness of who He is, meaning that you talk to Him, you ask His opinion, you pray with Him for help, and you have seen or have been used by the Holy Spirit to heal others and set them free, you are missing out on the greatest power of God you can experience! But you are also not operating in the fullness of who you are. And with the freedom in Christ that you, if you're like me, are desiring. I would encourage you to ask the Holy Spirit today, what you can do to build a better relationship with Him and then listen for His answer. It might be a voice in your head, a feeling, a song on the radio that means something. For me, when the Holy Spirit is present, it brings me to tears.

During this time, God used the Holy Spirit to teach me, convict me, and advise me on how to respond to things and what to do about some of the choices I was faced with having to have answers to. I began to ask the Holy Spirit as many times a day as I could remember what I should do or what I was seeing or experiencing when things seemed off, but also in everyday experiences. Today, the Holy Spirit is an active part of my day and conversations, as well as an encourager in how to really bring the power of God to ministry and healing the brokenhearted, which we will again explore in later chapters. But one of the most prevalent ways He ministered to me during this time was through prophecy. He pointed me to prophetic training and to people who have the gift of prophecy and began to place me in churches where their goal was to empower people in their gifts and how to steward those gifts well.

As I've mentioned, I was never taught the power of the Holy Spirit and the authority that we all carry as believers in Christ in the same way that I know about these things now. I cannot read the Bible now without seeing all the scriptures that reference "in the Spirit," many that were goalposts for me, and I had no idea I would never "achieve" without the power of the Holy Spirit, like being able to enjoy the fruit of the Spirit. Don't get me wrong, in hindsight, the Holy Spirit was always there, but not in the same way it is now. And I'm sad I didn't get to experience that fullness for much of my life. But now that I know, I can't go backward! And prophecy is a great tool to have that can help you and others to move forward. Prophesy is God's way of connecting His thoughts, design for your life and His love for you, today.

In Corinthians 14:1, "Follow the way of love and eagerly desire gifts of the Spirit, especially prophecy." In my experience, I watched people pray over others who would ask the Holy Spirit what that person needed to hear or heal from and then they would repeat it to the person. I received my first prophetic word in 2019 and the power of some of the words I received I still remember, and they drive me to keep going. I also sought out multiple training events and even hosted one of my own just before closing the ministry. Here are the key takeaways. First, we can all prophesy by asking the Holy Spirit. Second, the purpose is to build up, meaning encourage and build the faith, of the church and its members. And third, the recipient is as responsible for the word as the one giving it. If the word does not resonate with you, don't receive it. For me, when the words are accurate, I can feel the word deep in my soul and some of those early words brought so much clarity and hope to me as they spoke to things, I had never said out loud yet regarding some of the abusive behavior and experiences.

I will continue to reveal more things that I have learned and am still learning today about prophecy, but I wanted to introduce it here. Hearing from others about God's heart confirming what we've heard from Him helps us know that He is still there, and we matter. In 2 Timothy 1:6-7 it says "For this reason I remind you to fan into flame the gift of God, which is in you through the laying on of my hands. For the Spirit God gave us does not make us timid, but gives us power, love, and self-discipline." It is much easier to understand God's ways when you are in relationship with Him through the Holy Spirit! If you desire more of the Holy Spirit, ask Him. He knows what you need and what you can handle.

Relative to the time when I began learning more about the Holy Spirit, God also reconciled the dreams I had once had as a young adult and helped me to see that they were and are a gift. In a similar way, He reconciled the gift of speaking in tongues, because I had seen it manipulated to force a belief or control of myself and others. For some denominations, especially the charismatic ones, there is a belief that the gift of speaking in tongues is automatic when you receive the Holy Spirit. As such, there is a converse belief in some leaders that if you don't speak in tongues that you do not have the Holy Spirit in you, resulting in a forced persistence to get it quickly! I asked the Holy Spirit to help me have trust in the gift of tongues before He gave it to me. I can now testify that my prayers, especially when I don't know what to pray, are more effective than without the gift.

Finally, I didn't learn that there was a family legacy of dreams, visions, preaching and leading until the healing portion of my journey, which I will share in future chapters. However, I had always known that my voice was loud in the spirit. I had no idea then why that was or how I understood that, but I now know it was the Holy Spirit in me. People would regularly ask me for advice, and I knew things others didn't know. I had wisdom beyond my age. And I had dreams and visions about futuristic things. I was in my early twenties when the dreams started. They would continue well into my later twenties and always included a catastrophic major event. In the dreams I was always floating over a catastrophe, almost like an angel, and I would console the victims and show them the way to heaven. The last dream I had like that was the Northridge earthquake in Los Angeles in 1994. I dreamt of the devastation, and because we had lived there at one point in our lives, we still had friends there, and I warned one of them in particular about what I had dreamt. The next day the earthquake hit. I had no idea, because of my traditional, conservative upbringing, that these types of dreams had a prophetic purpose. So I asked God to take them away, and He did. I have not had a dream with a future catastrophic event like that since then, though I have asked God to return them to me when I'm ready to steward them better. Regardless, I have always had and still do have regular dreams and visions from God that have a specific purpose in showing me what He wants me to hear and know from Him, as well as dreams that are warnings, sometimes futuristic, and prophetic for others.

What I now know is that women carry a unique authority in the Spirit to discern evil and hear from God through the Holy Spirit, which is why it is one of the reasons Satan focuses his attacks on women. Jesus came to us as a result of an immaculate conception with the Holy Spirit and Mary. He then had women in His circle, advocated on their behalf, and included them in His plans. Women were in the upper room when the Holy Spirit fell on the disciples and women were the first to see Him as he arose, and they too were empowered by the Holy Spirit to speak on His behalf. And the Holy Spirit is alive and well today so that you can talk to Him, ask Him your questions, and seek Him out when you need a counselor, advocate, helper, and friend. And maybe the most extraordinary function of the Holy Spirit, especially for women, is help us to live in freedom and hear from God directly.

Reflection

1. How have you ever considered that the Holy Spirit is a different relationship with God than Jesus? How is it different for you?
2. Can you think of times that the Holy Spirit was an Advocate to you? A Counselor? A Helper? Given you legal counsel?
3. In what ways are you able to walk in peace because of the Holy Spirit?
4. How does the Holy Spirit help you exhibit the attributes of the fruit of the Spirit?
5. What beliefs have you allowed to get in the way from recognizing the spiritual gifts, including the gift of prophecy, to stop you from pursuing them?

CHAPTER 5

THE POWER OF HER PROPHETIC IDENTITY

"For you created my inmost being, you knit me together in my mother's womb. I praise you because I am fearfully and wonderfully made; your works are wonderful; I know that full well."

—PSALM 139:13–14

The power of Your prophetic identity is understanding who God says you are, knowing that He designed you intentionally and exactly the way you are and that no one else can be or do what you can. Now that I had a better understanding of what was happening to me during my last ministry season, and how Jesus really feels and demonstrated His love for women during His time on earth, it was time for Him to restore my identity and purpose. Identity, of course, has so many components to it, but He wanted me to focus on the ones that He gives us and guides us to walk in. Identity isn't just who we are personally; it's also how we function and is the foundation that leads to what purposes we can't help but pursue, how we lead and influence others, and how we are uniquely qualified to do that one thing that only we can do. In the business world, we call that our "unfair advantage," the thing that makes us unique. And because God always starts my journeys with a dream, you won't be surprised when I tell you that this process started the same. During a dream, He started showing me that our identity and the process we go through to get there is one of the many blueprints found in His Word. He said that He would show me the blueprint and asked that I share it in this book. Within a week of the dream, a stranger gave me a prophetic word that I would develop a "model" that helps people discover, establish, and restore when needed, their identity, purpose, leadership assignments, and calling. That model, which I call the P.I.N.K. framework, is the represented by each chapter of the book, including the ones you just read.

The power of your prophetic identity lies in your relationship with God, and it is His power that allows you to overcome what the world is bringing your way and helps you operate authentically in who He designed you to be. But His power is blocked when your identity is disrupted by you or someone else, not allowing you to reach the fullness of His design. For me, the limiting beliefs around women, both those of others and my own, were the disruptor, and my agreement with it is what allowed it to change me. But there also seemed to be more to it than that. Many people in ministry had their own operating systems with their own rules and own language, creating a certain culture that I didn't seem to fit well in. Though I understood from my business experience how to create a corporate culture and how roles could be different in a company, sometimes causing conflict, this culture seemed more hardwired in that people were doing it without understanding they were. As God allowed me to experience many expressions of the whole Church, He placed in me an understanding of how He designed each of us individually and uniquely and reassured me this was *good*. Then He helped me see how we all fit together corporately and pointed me to scripture that confirmed what He was equipping me with. He taught me to look at each member of the body and say, "that's good" and recognize that while each of us has a process to go through with Him to be refined, our role as believers is to help build up the body of Christ, not tear it down.

It is through our diversity that we are one body of believers, with each part being as important as the rest. The Church is also an ecosystem. We were not designed to have one leader while the rest of us follow. We were all designed to do our part as believers, interdependent of each other, meaning what I do affects you and what you do affects me. So you are becoming established in your own identity, purpose, leadership assignments, and calling doesn't just affect you; it affects your family, your community, and the Church. Now that God had placed all of this new understanding in me, showing it to me in His Word, I needed to know how to put the blueprint together for others to see.

What I didn't know until much later in my own journey was that God was walking me through a process the entire time. Part of that process was to give me the unsettled feeling and the holy irritation so that I would begin to seek Him out for guidance. He then began to refine and restore me. But He started by bringing truth about what the journey was about, who He is, and how I'm designed, while He exposed some of the lies, I had been believed, and activated the power of the Holy Spirit in my life to help change my perspective and activate a greater level of faith in me.

The P.I.N.K. framework represents how to discover and establish the attributes that make up our Prophetic identity, Incubated purpose, Nurtured leadership, and Kingdom calling. These components of the framework are how God sees you and how He helps you become empowered to be the person He designed you to be and do the things He placed in you a desire to do. In other words, they are in you, but you need Jesus and the Holy Spirit to help you bring them out in their fullness. At some point, often simultaneously, you begin to develop your purpose, discover your spiritual gifts, have discernment over the things that become part of your journey, and if you are stepping out in ministry in any way, you will begin to experience spiritual warfare and have to respond to it in a healthier way. These things are established through prophecy, meaning other people in the Church are speaking to them into your life.

As a result of establishing your prophetic identity and allowing God and others to incubate your purpose, God will equip and nurture you into leadership assignments and your kingdom calling in the way that God designed you to. Your leadership assignments help restore all of the things you have experienced along the way, allow you step into your own mantles from others or assignments that he has for you, give you the freedom to create and innovate new things and have new ideas, and ultimately, develop your voice and your message. But this step is often one of the hardest as it is often accomplished alone and is a refining process. This process is referred to as the refining fire and is meant to equip and establish you to launch into your calling. At this point, your focus should be the Kingdom (God's larger body and His plan to reconcile all of us to Him for eternity). And your focus should be how you fit into the entire body of Christ and how to do things God's way using His principles and plans.

Additionally, as you become activated by the Holy Spirit into your prophetic identity; into your incubated purpose through prophecy; and your nurtured leadership through the refining fire; the outcome is your testimony, reconciliation, an ecosystem of believers that complement your calling, your ability to create blueprints and becoming anointed to complete the work, that God has given you to do in unity with others.

P.I.N.K. FRAMEWORK

PROPHETIC IDENTITY	INCUBATED PURPOSE	NURTURED LEADERSHIP	KINGDOM CALLING
HER JOURNEY	HER SPIRITUAL WARFARE	HER RESTORATION	HER RECONCILIATION
HER TRUTH	HER DISCERNMENT	HER MANTLES	HER ECOSYSTEM
HER DESIGN	HER SPIRITUAL GIFTS	HER INNOVATION	HER BLUEPRINTS
HER SPIRIT	HER AUTHORITY	HER VOICE	HER ANOINTING
ACTIVATED BY HOLY SPIRIT	ACTIVATED BY PROPHESY	ESTABLISHED BY FIRE	ESTABLISHED IN UNITY

The framework is designed so that you can go through this process yourself, using this book and some of the resources in the back of the book. As you are going through this process, keep in mind that it is a process, and it is not necessarily going to present itself fully right away. If you have trauma or experiences from your past that still need to be processed or healed, you might have to dig deeper over time as you move closer to God's design. As I went through this process myself, and still am going through it, I've thought to myself at times that I have finally arrived, only to realize that there's more. I'm not sure we ever finally arrive! But we can grow enough to experience freedom, gain wisdom, and have peace with who we are. Additionally, because the body of Christ is interdependent, you may need help from others with some of the sections. This is a great exercise to do in groups, with people you have some familiarity with or with people gifted in prophecy, as they will be able to point out things you may or may not see for yourself.

As you can see you have begun the process already. The first part of your Prophetic Identity is to reconcile your journey. The second is to seek out the truth that you need to adjust in your life. The third is your design and the fourth is to build a relationship with the Holy Spirit. This is what that looked like for me. God needed to build me back up in my own identity and for me, what was missing was Him. I desperately needed to know how He saw me, as opposed to man. But I also needed to understand what He said about my journey, the truth in His Word and His design for me. And finally, in order to see these things, I needed more of the Holy Spirit. But as I began to see, hear, and know more from the Holy Spirit, God also began to show me that some of the things I had experienced were not just from people behaving badly, but were in partnership with the enemy, and the true author of many of the things that I experienced.

Reflection

1. What parts of your Identity have been disrupted because of believing the wrong things?
2. What themes both good or bad have you seen repeated over and over again? What can you do to change that?
3. What spiritual legacy do you have that you can regain and grow in?
4. How can you trust God more knowing that now the way that He designed you?
5. What pain points do you have that create passion in you to help others overcome?

CHAPTER 6

THE POWER OF HER SPIRITUAL WARFARE

"For our struggle is not against flesh and blood, but against the rulers, against the authorities, against the powers of this dark world and against the spiritual forces of evil in the heavenly realms."

—EPHESIANS 6:12

The power of your spiritual warfare is that it builds in you the tools and confidence in God to know beyond a reasonable doubt that He is there for you. The true author of the lies I believed was Satan, and he is the true enemy we are fighting. But since I had no understanding of how he operates, targeting believers of Jesus to do his work, I wasn't looking for his influence in the Church. It doesn't justify what some in the Church are doing to shut down women, but it does provide the bigger picture so we can address the root of the evil. One of the enemy's main objectives on earth is to get you and I to believe his lies about our identity, purpose, and God, so that we give up and walk away from one or all of those things.

I had read the same scriptures that I'm sure you've read about Satan. But I was taught those scriptures in a similar way that I was taught about the Holy Spirit, that it was this thing that existed but not anything tangible. I was also taught that Satan couldn't harm me or have access to me as a believer and not to worry about him too much. So, when I got hit with what I now understand was spiritual warfare, I had no clue what was happening to me. I went from having a happy middle-class life with no drama to all hell breaking loose around us. What I now understand, with a painstaking amount of detail, is that Satan can and does unleash his strategies against believers and the Church. And he does it through sin, not always the big ones we hear about from the pulpit and often categorize as the most egregious, but the ones we all commit and rarely think twice about: gossip, slander, pride, backbiting, etc. And because I participated in it and received the lies as truth, I unknowingly partnered with Satan's tactics, and I was not equipped at all to handle what I'd stepped into. I have now watched many leaders and churches get caught up in similar attacks that have resulted in major immoral and at times criminal behaviors. And while the Bible is clear there is a process for restoring people, we're all still responsible for the consequences of our own choices.

From 2009-2017 as the nonprofit ministry began to grow, not just in its governing board, staff, and volunteers, but also in its capacity and building, the team and I were hit so hard with every kind of crazy scenario that you can imagine and no understanding of the authority we had to stop it. The team who had been highly successful up to this point, literally became toxic seemingly overnight, not completing the work out of confusion over the assignments, backbiting, stirring up conflict and completely missing each other when communicating. It definitely felt like someone or something else was manipulating the behaviors as they were so out of the norm. I described it at the time like I was watching a movie that I was the star of but had no control over the outcome! I could not explain it, except to label it spiritual warfare and accept it if I wanted to participate in ministry, which is what the pastors in my circle suggested I do. The truth is my only experience with spiritual warfare at that point was to use the term to describe when things did not go my way, but I had no understanding that the enemy really can manipulate your circumstances. I just knew that circumstances seemed unreal and difficult to explain in worldly terms. Additionally, I was taught by the pastors in my circle that if the negative circumstances continued, then it meant God did not bless the work, which actually perpetuated shame and more sin, and I went on to attempt to do more, strive more, and be more perfect so that I could please God. As a result, these attacks not only increased in frequency but in size the entire nonprofit ministry season until 2017 when the Holy Spirit began to reveal the source of those attacks and helped me understand how I was perpetuating them to continue. And he pointed me to the names of the demonic spirits and their strategies and equipped me with understanding of the authority I had to defend myself or the team against them.

I know now that we didn't just get hit with one type of attack, but I and the team were attacked over and over again with a combination of demonic spirits and strategies in different ways. What I also now understand is that individual sin multiplies as it targets more individuals, your family circle and in my case a city or a region. The first attack came just six months after the nonprofit launch, losing over half of my board, all my family's personal finances for the year, and almost losing our family home. Many members of the nonprofit board also had their lives turned upside down including discovery of instances of sexual molestation, substance abuse, moral failures, financial indiscretions, and other crimes, all of which could be explained in a worldly way, but the frequency and timing all of it all coming out at once was overwhelming. In addition, the behaviors surrounding the situations included confusion, accusation, manipulation, gossip, an inability to communicate clearly or work things out often forgetting the conversations altogether, and deception. And these things were almost always carried out by believers who by outward appearances exercised peace, patience, understanding, kindness, gentleness, and self-control, but behind the scenes it was a different story.

One overall strategy that we saw in the nonprofit ministry, was when believers would approach the ministry wanting to partner or secure a job. Their tactic was to use flattery and the facade of like-mindedness in purpose, to obtain the position but once in the organization and secured in their position, then to methodically take it down through division and accusation. If you are a businessperson, you have likely seen this and labeled it the "toxic employee." But I now recognize the behavior as demonic strategy used to take the ministry down. And it works perfectly in the Church because everyone wants to be kind and exhibit the fruit of the Holy Spirit, which is good. At the same time, when the strategy partners with sin and bad behavior, it's easy to get mad at and point to the person alone, instead of understanding the author of it. One of the principles I learned is that the enemy always brings a false version of God's version. So, if you are unsuspecting, you won't recognize it, because it will look so much like God. In the Church today, where pastors preach grace but often refuse to have tough conversations or go through a reconciliation process to work through differences, especially when it's between a woman and a man, it leaves believers fighting amongst each other and issues of sin or offense never getting worked out. But the truth is, if you're getting caught up in the offense, you have played exactly into Satan's hands! He wants to keep you there so you're understanding ends blaming fellow believers in the world instead of your authority to shut down what is really going on.

The first step to understanding spiritual warfare is to understand that it does exist and that the strategies Satan uses are identifiable through Scripture and through behaviors. The second step is to get healed yourself, so you are not part of the problem. And the third step is to become equipped with the tools to recognize the attacks and respond to them better, through God's Word and the Holy Spirit. After a considerable amount of studying the Bible and having God connect me to ministries, I would have never listened to prior to my nonprofit experience, I came to understand that there were five main demonic strategies we were dealing with, as well as a fifth one that hit me personally. (Note: because God almost always gives me understanding first and then confirms what He gives me in His Word and others, I am not directly quoting others. However, there were many influences that I want to point you to that are great resources to the things I'm saying, and I wanted to source them here.)[7] These strategies included the spirit of religion, the political spirit, the spirit of fraternity, the Ahab and Jezebel spirits that can work separately but in my case were always together, and the leviathan spirit. The one that attacked me personally was a spirit of infirmity. Each one of these spirits has its own distinct set of behaviors, but they also often work together in different ways for different situations. And though God allowed us to experience these attacks, He also protected us. At the same time, though I wanted to quit and return to non-ministry settings and purposes, God placed a longing in my heart and stomach that I could not ignore or pray away, which kept me going. I knew He was asking me to stick with it and let Him train me in the way He wanted me to go.

This "devil doesn't exist" Baptist girl was beginning to think I was crazy! And I was becoming so defensive with the elevated attacks that were allowed to grow because of my underlying belief system, I had lost all trust in most people. I now understand that the underlying belief system itself is indicative of the religious spirit and the way it was carried out in some of our projects correlated to the political spirit. And that those two foundational spirits of religion and politics, allowed the other spirits and principalities to flourish and grow not just in my own circumstances but for many other ministry leaders in California. So by the time the nonprofit ministry was hitting its stride in 2016 and looked like we were going to really begin to make a significant difference in Sacramento, I found myself seemingly being targeted by leaders who wanted to partner with the ministry but for the wrong reasons. And their approach always had a similar look, with a man leading and a woman manipulating things behind the scenes. The man always said the words, "God called me to help you further your vision", which of course was my heart's desire, that men and women could work together. But then, after expressing his loyalty to me he would insist on my loyalty to him, requesting that I place him in a position of authority. And then the woman would show up to create chaos and distrust, through backbiting, accusation, and splitting—saying one thing to me and a completely opposite thing to others until my authority and voice were completely gone. I now know this is a classic Ahab and Jezebel spirit whose assignment is to take the leader and the ministry down. And I now understand that the people partnering with the enemy would often not remember things they had done afterward and refuse to try to work things out, believing they had done nothing wrong and that I was somehow imagining the conflict. Honestly, at first, I did think I was imagining it, but after this same scenario happened repeatedly with the same tactics, I knew it was more than me having a bad day. I have now witnessed these spirits and strategies attack and destroy many people, ministries, and churches. Prior to this experience, If you would have shared any of these types of stories with me and told me they were spiritual warfare, I would have not only questioned their veracity, but I would also have questioned your theology. In fact, I recently met with a friend who has now gone through a similar experience to mine, and she said that if she didn't know me and been through her own version of my story herself now, she would have a hard time believing all of the crazy things I went through. So let's go to the Bible where you will not only find that Satan can do these things, but where you will also find these demonic spirits and their strategies, as I did.

First, let's start with what Satan can and can't do. In Job 1 we learn that God does allow Satan to test us as well as manipulate and lie to us. In Job 2 we see how Satan infected Job with a skin disease in order to afflict him, and we learn that he roams the earth. In Colossians 2:14 we see that while he can make accusations and try to charge us with legal indebtedness, Christ has freed us from this and he can't see it through, without our agreement. In Matthew 4, we read that he does not know the future but that there is a geographical and governmental nature to the kingdoms of the world, of which he is the ruler. In 1 Peter 5:8–9, we learn that he can cause suffering: "Be alert and of sober mind. Your enemy the devil prowls around like a roaring lion looking for someone to devour. Resist him, standing firm in the faith, because you know that the family of believers throughout the world is undergoing the same kind of sufferings." And in 2 Corinthians 12:6–9 we learn that God allowed Satan to torment Paul: "Even if I should choose to boast, I would not be a fool, because I would be speaking the truth. But I refrain, so no one will think more of me than is warranted by what I do or say, or because of these surpassingly great revelations. Therefore, in order to keep me from becoming conceited, I was given a thorn in my flesh, a messenger of Satan, to torment me. Three times I pleaded with the Lord to take it away from me. But he said to me, 'My grace is sufficient for you, for my power is made perfect in weakness. Therefore I will boast all the more gladly about my weaknesses, so that Christ's power may rest on me.'" Finally, in Revelation 12:10 we read that Satan will be defeated and, in the future, will be unable to bring guilty sentences upon Christians, which suggests he can do that now. This, of course, is not an exhaustive list of scripture that refers to the enemy's strategies against God's people, but it is the ones most relevant for this discussion. I would encourage you to study these scriptures for yourself.

Now let's break down some of the specific spirits found in Scripture that I experienced in my own journey and that are common in other women's journeys as well. The underlying spirit that is driving the attack on women is the spirit of religion. The spirit of religion takes what is in the Bible and twists it to fit the narrative or position that one is trying to further. The hardest part about being on the receiving end of this is that there is truth in what the person is saying, but not the whole truth, which is why we have to know the truths in the Bible for ourselves. In Galatians 1:6–8, Paul exhorts the Galatians, "I am astonished that you are so quickly deserting the one who called you to live in the grace of Christ and are turning to a different gospel—which is really no gospel at all. Evidently some people are throwing you into confusion and are trying to pervert the gospel of Christ. But even if we or an angel from heaven should preach a gospel other than the one, we preached to you, let them be under God's curse!" Galatians is a great place to start any study on the religious spirit. In my experience, I engaged in the religious spirit by agreeing with the lies that I was not good enough and that I had to be perfect to please God, being rigid about the rules and striving to do more and more good works, and of course in believing that God would not call me as a woman! The way churches participate in the spirit of religion is insisting that those things are part of Jesus's expectations, requiring that women have to do what men require them to do even when it's not what's good for them, and participating in legalism, religious pride, and self-righteousness. Other behaviors that can position Christians to partner with this spirit are listed in Galatians 5:19: "sexual immorality, lustful thoughts, pornography, chasing after things instead of God, manipulating others, hating those who get in your way, senseless arguments, resentment when others are favored, temper tantrums, angry quarrels, only thinking of yourself, being in love with your own opinions, being envious of the blessings of others, murder, uncontrolled addictions, wild parties and other similar behavior".

The political spirit is motivated by greed, money, and power, specifically to bind others with political ideologies, laws, and governance. The spirit operates by wooing others to believe that they are working for the person's good (i.e., they try to sound like God) but has a hidden agenda and operates in the root of pride. Early on in my season in ministry, I was blessed to meet a man by the name of Tom White, the author of many books on this topic, including *The Believers Guide to Spiritual Warfare*. Tom has spent his life traveling the world in prayer movements and witnessing and writing down how the enemy operates and usually succeeds in stopping church movements. I will never forget him warning a group of us early on that there is a particular spirit and strategy that operates in capital cities across the world, and the goal of this spirit is to shut down moves of God in that region. He told us the counter strategy to breaking that spirit is to put everything in writing. I remember the Holy Spirit that day highlighting to me that I should hang on to that wisdom. I have never forgotten it! And though he never called it the political spirit, when I witnessed it, I knew that was it.

The political spirit often operates in partnership with the religious spirit. The political spirit is the same spirit Jesus dealt with in His day with the Pharisees. The political spirit is also a false religion that worships power and money. When believers and churches partner with this spirit, they become subject to the sin nature that comes with it. When you see churches partnering with government elites for the purpose of gaining power, money, and attention for their ministry or church, you're watching the political spirit at play. I'm not saying you can never partner with a government entity to do good. I'm saying when you do, and especially when you do it for the purpose of gaining power, control, and finances, you must be careful not to replace God with the gods of power and greed. The purpose of the political spirit is to get you to first partner with it out of hurt or financial need but then entangle you into its system so that you become indebted to it and unable to operate your ministry without that spirit and its influence.

The spirit of fraternity was the next spirit and the one that I had recognized most of my life that encompassed many of the limiting behaviors including the secret meetings, the agreement to not discuss the limiting belief system with women and the creation of policies that keeps women out of high-level meetings by saying that men and women cannot meet together for fear of appearances or worst, sexual misconduct. The spirit of fraternity also speaks to the secret meeting of the group of men who first coined the term complementarianism and their efforts to continue to define narrowly women's role in culture, as well as attach it to a political agenda to force it's acceptance. First, I have to say that for men to believe that just because men and women are working together, them being in a room together will result in sexual relations, is a sure sign of poor health in both the leaders and the person! When I first opened our coworking space, a very healthy leader noticed early on that all of the doors to the offices in our space were wooden and did not have windows. So we hired someone to put windows into every door so that there was no question who was in the room and that their behaviors were above board. Pretty simple solution! When the Holy Spirit dropped the spirit of fraternity in my spirit, my initial reaction was "yes, that describes it perfectly". And then, He revealed it to me in Scripture.

A fraternity according to Merriam Webster is "a group of people associated or formally organized for a common purpose, interest, or pleasure, the quality or state of being brothers, or persons of the same class, profession, character, or tastes."[8] And all of these things can be good and are spoke of highly in regard to how the community of believers could be together. The Holy Spirit though began to highlight a few things to me. First, why did Jesus fairly often call the Pharisees hypocrites? And what exactly was a Pharisee? Wikipedia describes the pharisees as a "fraternal society" who defined themselves around their version of belief system and then created religious prescriptions around their beliefs. And further says, "The New Testament, particularly the Synoptic Gospels, presents especially the leadership of the Pharisees as obsessed with man-made rules (especially concerning purity) whereas Jesus is more concerned with God's love; the Pharisees scorn sinners whereas Jesus seeks them out." Jesus says in Matthew 23:13, "Woe to you, teachers of the law and Pharisees, you hypocrites! You shut the door of the kingdom of heaven in people's faces. You yourselves do not enter, nor will you let those enter who are trying to." The spirit of fraternity is founded in secret agreements, rituals, rules, and often Biblical beliefs that are set apart to fit the narrative of the group with an underlying behavior of pride and desire for more power and control. They were right and everyone else was wrong. They made vows to support their beliefs. They created laws around their beliefs condemning those that did not follow. I.e. the woman who was to be stoned. Then they defined it with politics. They're laws coupled with the secrecy, and being set apart from others making their set of beliefs right while everyone else is wrong is a false religion. Paul was set a part, as a member of this group, to change and graft in the Gentiles. This was why Jesus' came and changed the culture!

The next type of spirit, the spirit of Ahab and Jezebel, is fueled by the underlying spirits of religion and politics, and is a demonic network released to create a web of confusion, always using witchcraft (the worship of false gods) to take down your ministry. Jezebel in particular is fueled by rejection and sexual abuse or assault, making women particularly susceptible to its attack. While the behavior of Jezebel is alarming, when it is used as an accusation against a strong woman, the agreement with the lie, creates a partnership with the spirit and curses both the accuser and the accused. Jezebel often presents herself as an intercessor but in action she is a gossip spreading, and information-seeking spirit. She (or he) is not seeking the information so they can pray and see God intervene, they are seeking information to prey on your hurts and wounds. But they often go undetected because they portray themselves as holy and pure, spreading lies and false agendas. As Proverbs 18:21 says, "The tongue has the power of life and death, and those who love it will eat its fruit." The story of King Ahab and his wife, Jezebel, is depicted in 1 Kings 21:17. When Jezebel married Ahab, she convinced him to institute worship of nature, in particular the gods of Baal, and to destroy anyone who opposed this, which included God's prophets. Elijah prophesied that God would send a drought as divine retribution to her demand that the people worship false gods, and he later killed the Baal priests. Jezebel promised to have Elijah killed. Though Elijah had just defeated the false gods, he ran from Jezebel, agreeing with the lie that she could defeat him despite him knowing that no one could thwart Gods plans or God himself.

The Jezebel spirit often works in tandem with an Ahab spirit, which is exemplified by someone who comes across as gentle, kind, and agreeable in nature. But behind him is usually a Jezebel pulling the strings and telling him what to do. It's a good front so that deceit will be allowed, especially in the church, where the kind, gentle, and agreeable behavior is rewarded. Though the two spirits can operate individually or as either male or female, the way I've seen it operate most is with a male representing Ahab and a female representing Jezebel. The Jezebel spirit causes people to control, intimidate, manipulate, and make allegations against other Christians, keeping them in bondage. The Jezebel spirit can be seen in situations that include sex trafficking, control in marriages or relationships, divorce, same-sex relationships, pornography, and adultery. The Jezebel spirit works most effectively through gossip and slander, splitting up groups and excluding certain people from the group because they are not righteous enough. I've also seen this spirit work by striving to be in control of any ministry where there was a public face to it or demanding to be the only ministry that received funds from churches, then misusing those funds for selfish and personal gain. The Jezebel spirit is often attached to very visible ministries, even prayer and worship ministries, that insist on having all the attention. A sure way to discern this duo at work is to try to partner with them in any meaningful way; then, when you get below the surface, you'll find the truth is not what has been presented. The evidence is not hard to find if you're looking, but most in the Church don't bother to look. Again, the world often sees it, but the Church rarely does, which continues to undermine the integrity of the Church and affect who enters the kingdom of God.

One of the reasons that the Church has been lulled into tolerating the Jezebel spirit is because of the Ahab spirit. The two are partnered equally and together, but often the man will be given grace while the woman is blamed for the behaviors. Appeasing these behaviors and doing nothing to stop them will continue to fuel these spirits, which can and do take down entire ministries and regions when they are tolerated. The number one sign of someone operating in the spirit of religion or Jezebel is their refusal to walk through any type of reconciliation meeting when they have wronged others. Additionally, you will notice they move from church to church repeating their sinful behavior, until they get what they need from a church or become "discovered" in their behavior. Again, their goal is to take down the ministry, church, or leadership. I've seen this spirit operate in the Church too many times to mention. And as the Jezebel Spirit continues to find fertile ground that she can work with in a church, city, or region, she will create a powerful web of destruction that is hard to break. When that happens, it becomes part of the larger strategy in that area and can be seen as a prevailing demonic entity that operates in all areas of culture.

Finally, the spirit of leviathan is a powerful principality that gets fueled by all the other underlying spirits. In other words, as the other spirits are ignored and the behaviors not dealt with, the web of Jezebel and the principality of leviathan becomes the ruling spirit. It is the same spirit that Job dealt with and tried everything to shut down. The more he tried, the worse it got, leading him to the realization that it was so powerful, only God could destroy it. Isaiah 27:1 says, "In that day, the LORD will punish with his sword, his fierce, great, and powerful sword, leviathan the gliding serpent, leviathan the coiling serpent; he will slay the monster of the sea." This principality creates bondage as it orchestrates other demonic spirits to take down leaders who love Jesus but are operating in pride and a posture of being right.

The stronghold establishes a system of thoughts that all work together to unleash custom strategies to different people and organizations, ensuring they don't succeed in God's plans. One of those custom strategies that was unleashed on me was the spirit of infirmity.

The enemy knew that I had struggled as a young adult with weight and the underlying issues of feeling I was not good enough, loved, or in control of my own life experiences. This resulted in excessive dieting, poor body image, and eventually bulimia. I had dealt with those things early in life, or so I thought, until they were brought back into view as I started the ministry, gaining over fifty pounds in the first six months. I responded by exercising and dieting more, but those things did not work this time. I went to multiple doctors, all of whom said they didn't know why I was gaining weight. In Luke 13:1–12 we read, "And a woman was there who had been crippled by a spirit for eighteen years. She was bent over and could not straighten up at all. When Jesus saw her, he called her forward and said to her, 'Woman, you are set free from your infirmity.'" For me even now, this ongoing struggle with weight is a present reality. While I know that the spirit is no longer keeping me in bondage, I still have to deal with the residual damage and am contending with God for complete healing. The spirit of infirmity will go after your body and mind, through illnesses, addiction, and both physical and mental responses to sin. Some of the symptoms of this spiritual attack involve torment, nervousness, anxiety, tension, headaches, anger, heart palpitations, vomiting, and autoimmune conditions where your body is literally attacking itself.

Over time, I learned to recognize the red flags of spiritual warfare and understand what was happening. If I am in a conversation today and my words start getting twisted or we started going in circles, I now recognize it is the leviathan spirit trying to shut down my voice. I now know that if a man and a woman are entangling me in their own conflict, one exhibiting kindness while the other is mean spirited and literally evil in the behavior, I know that's the Ahab and Jezebel spirits at play. If I suddenly am faced with behavior that is rigid and lacking grace, unusual amounts of profanity, or control around a religious concept or statement, I know that's the spirit of religion often mixed with witchcraft which we will discuss further in future chapters. I often see the political spirit in our capital region trying to partner with the Church in unhealthy ways to get Christians to agree to the strings attached to their finances or projects. Finally, I now know that when my body is under attack and gets inflamed just at the moment that I'm breaking through on a book or a project, it is the spirit of infirmity being used to stop me in an assignment or my calling. Unfortunately, much of what you will experience will be so targeted to fit you, it will be hard for you to recognize right away what spirit is at work. But the Holy Spirit will guide you.

Whew, that was an intense topic! But now the good part. What I now know is that I could have addressed many of the things that happened to me differently, and I would have seen much better outcomes. I now understand that I have as much authority over them as men do. The simplest response to any attack is to be sure you and the people around you are not partnering with any of it through your own sin. Start by apologizing and asking God for forgiveness for anything you have done to partner with the behavior. Then pray for the people, including yourself, who are part of the attack. Resist getting mad, angry, or bitter, and then complaining about it through gossip or backbiting. That will just fuel the enemy and ensure the attacks will continue.

And put on the armor of God! I have a dear friend who started calling or texting me every morning during this season to be sure that I had on my spiritual armor. Once I learned to read God's Word through a lens of grace and best practices, instead of as a rule book (spirit of religion), I realized that all of His Word was for my good. Ephesians 6:10–18 says to put on the armor of God every day to be sure you're protected against the enemy:

Put on the full armor of God, so that you can take your stand against the devil's schemes. For our struggle is not against flesh and blood, but against the rulers, against the authorities, against the powers of this dark world and against the spiritual forces of evil in the heavenly realms. Therefore put on the full armor of God, so that when the day of evil comes, you may be able to stand your ground, and after you have done everything, to stand. Stand firm then, with the belt of truth buckled around your waist, with the breastplate of righteousness in place, and with your feet fitted with the readiness that comes from the gospel of peace. In addition to all this, take up the shield of faith, with which you can extinguish all the flaming arrows of the evil one. Take the helmet of salvation and the sword of the Spirit, which is the word of God. And pray in the Spirit on all occasions with all kinds of prayers and requests. With this in mind, be alert and always keep on praying for all the Lord's people.

God's Word is a blueprint for the Church. The blueprint can be a set of rules much like the Pharisees handled the law. Or it can be over graced, resulting in enabling and keeping people bound. Or it can be a balance between truth and grace that the Bible gives us as best practices for any situation, but especially in warfare. The more rules-based churches say warfare doesn't exist. The over graced churches say it exists, but we don't need to do anything about it. And the balanced approach, which is consistent with Scripture, says we should expect it and gives us best practices on how to handle it. I can tell you without a doubt that spiritual warfare exists, and if you do nothing, it will not only persist but take your ministry down. While the Bible gives the Church a blueprint on how to be the Church and how to be different from the world, culture often influences the Church instead of the Church influencing culture. When the Church partners with culture on culture's terms, it often gets entangled with sin. And sin invites warfare. The systematic shutdown of women has all the markings of a leviathan spirit. And the intentional secret meetings and political partnerships forged in the 1980s to stop biblical feminism were doors that were opened and partnerships that were forged with the religious, political, fraternal, Ahab, Jezebel, and leviathan spirits, to release demonic strategies against women that fueled its power. But you have the authority to stop it and we need in the church need to reconcile it!

Reflection

1. Have you ever watched a scene happening and said to yourself, "This feels off"? What did you do about it?
2. Have you ever experienced a level of backbiting, gossip, and accusation that had no truth to it but somehow kept getting passed on? What was your response to it?
3. Have you ever suffered an illness the doctors could not explain? How did you resolve it?
4. Are you currently experiencing any situations in your own work or ministry that look similar to the ones I have described? Ask the Holy Spirit to discern now to respond.
5. What will you do differently now that you know that sin can open up a partnership with the enemy?

CHAPTER 7

THE POWER
OF HER
DISCERNMENT

*"The person without the Spirit does not accept the
things that come from the Spirit of God but consid-
ers them foolishness and cannot understand them because they are discerned only through the Spirit."*

—I CORINTHIANS 2:14

The power of discernment is the ability to judge well, to recognize God's will or to distinguish between what is morally or
spiritually right or wrong. The gift of discernment is a gift that many
women have and that others, especially the guys, often call our "gut
instinct". It is the reason that I have separated this spiritual gift into
its own chapter. When you discover how to discern the difference
between the motivation and the author of the behavior that you are

experiencing it will bring you an incredible amount of peace and the power to make decisions to let things go, pursue them in prayer or try and create change around the issue.

I now understand that I have always had the gift of discernment in me, but I didn't have language for it or know how to properly use the gift for the purposes it was designed. The gift of discernment is like all spiritual gifts and is given to us to build us and others up and to build up the Church. Early in my corporate business career I was employed as a special investigator in the insurance industry. My role was to investigate insurance claims that had "red flags" and the facts didn't seem to add up. I discovered early on that I had a gift for being able to tell when people were lying and getting them to confess their lies and tell the truth. As I progressed through the industry, I eventually spent every day of my workday reading piles and piles of documents, taking statements under oath from witnesses and claimants, to uncover the truth. I had almost a perfect success rate in getting confessions on fraud cases and suggesting the district attorney prosecute the cases. But my lens was always critical and looking for the worst in people! Eventually, that way of always looking at people for the lies, crept into my personal life and I developed a critical nature about people who wouldn't tell the truth. And honestly, it didn't make for a fun job after a while!

As I continued my journey and God revealed to me some of the truths that I have shared in the last chapters, and I was learning more about the Holy Spirit, I started to realize that my holy irritation was likely the result of my own internal process for recognizing that something wasn't right and wanting to discover the truth or the root of the issue. And that pursuit of the truth was on at an increased level for a while as I sorted things out. The greatest tool though that the Holy Spirit taught me during that time was to ask Him and discern correctly who the author of the behavior, deceit or manipulation was, man, Satan, or God. When man is involved, you will be able to discern that sin involved. If there is no outward sin involved, it's likely something the person has allowed in through their own free will, and they may not be aware of it. When this is the case, a conversation will resolve it. But, when the enemy is involved, it looks different. When you trying to resolve the issue with a conversation, the person will either refuse, twist the process, deflect, or say they've done nothing wrong and not have an understanding or memory of having said or done anything that deserves a conversation. And when God is involved, of course, you should expect to see the fruit of His outcomes as a result, and since Matthew 18 is one of His blueprints to help believers come to agreement, when they refuse to, it's a signal He's not in it.

The Scripture says to test every spirit. In the last chapter you saw that you have to know that the Holy Spirit is real to even believe that there is a spiritual component of our faith! If you believe in the words of the Bible only and not that those words are for today and active in our lives, then it will be more difficult to understand the things happening in your journey except to weigh them by earthly definitions and explanations. In 1 John 4:1-3 it says, "Dear friends, do not believe every spirit, but test the spirits to see whether they are from God, because many false prophets have gone out into the world. This is how you can recognize the Spirit of God: Every spirit that acknowledges that Jesus Christ has come in the flesh is from God, but every spirit that does not acknowledge Jesus, is not from God. This is the spirit of the antichrist, which you have heard is coming and even now is already in the world." This is where it is gets interesting. The scripture says that when you test the spirit the way to do it is to ask the spirit if it acknowledges Jesus is from God. The good news is that any person who loves God and acknowledges Jesus, the Holy Spirit lives in them. But so does a spirit of the flesh, sin. We will explore this much more as we progress but for me as a former investigator, and as the Holy Spirit starting training me in this, I started to recognize red flags that indicated to me when I should investigate further.

When I was a special investigator (by the way I'm still a licensed private investigator just for fun!), I would ask questions of people and hold them up to the truth of the law or the other information that I had developed before examining them. God developed in me a similar process using His Word as the truth to help confirm my discernment around spiritual things. First, I always ask myself if the behavior I'm witnessing or experiencing, is in Scripture and if it would affirm or deny it was acceptable. Second, I ask the Holy Spirit to discern what the motivation behind the behavior? Is it to build up the Church? Build themselves up? Or for some other nefarious reason? Third, to see if the outcomes of the behaviors are consistent with God's promises and demonstrate His fruit. Is the behavior harming people or helping them? Is it causing unity or division? Is it resulting in the fruit of the Spirit or sin? And last, is there truth to it but it's not exactly true? This last question, I discovered, is almost always how Satan operates.

As a woman, I have always had a gut reaction when leaders, especially in the church, would exhibit the limiting behaviors against women by shutting them down when they are talking or exerting unnecessary control over them for example. Something in me instinctually knew it was wrong. Many of you have likely had a similar experience but maybe you can't put words to why you feel it's wrong. So God began to have me process the behavior and hold it up to His Word as the truth, to see if it was from Him or someone else. Let's take some of the statements we hear at times and weigh it against the truth of God's Word. For example, I have had quite a few experiences where a person who exhibits bad behavior does so to protect a position or title that they have. This behavior would likely be a product of being human and choosing to behave badly for potentially selfish reasons. But I have also seen this type of behavior grow and spread to others through gossip creating a culture or an atmosphere of sin for others.

When a conversation does not resolve or stop the behavior from continuing, your next step is to look at the motivation behind the behavior and weigh it against what Scripture says is sin. Let me just say here, we all sin, and fall short! But again, the point is you cannot resolve it. In 1 John 3:6-10 it says, "No one who continues to sin has either seen him or known him. Dear children, do not let anyone lead you astray. The one who does what is right is righteous, just as he is righteous. The one who does what is sinful is of the devil, because the devil has been sinning from the beginning." Further, Scripture defines the behaviors you're looking for as the behaviors that come from the flesh, in Galatians 5:19-21, "Now the works of the flesh are evident: sexual immorality, impurity, sensuality, idolatry, sorcery, enmity, strife, jealousy, fits of anger, rivalries, dissensions, divisions, envy, drunkenness, orgies, and things like these. I warn you, as I warned you before, that those who do such things will not inherit the kingdom of God." We should all want to resolve issues amongst brothers and sisters and bring agreement, sometimes that agreement being to agree to disagree, but still being able to be in peace.

So, as I moved forward in my own journey, I used both discernment and the truths I've discussed above, to decide if I pursue trying to create change over the limiting belief system that I now understand held me back. So let's use the lenses above. First, does the belief system hold up to scripture? As you have seen in prior chapters, you can see that there is truth in Scripture where Paul advises churches around specific issues of women teaching men, staying silent and governing in the church. But nowhere in scripture or in Paul's words are these things to be applied as a universal prescription to women or to the church. I have my own opinion as to the underlying motivations of the Southern Baptist Convention regarding their decision to remove women as pastors and seemingly reverse their belief system, but I'll let them answer to that. What I can safely say is that the fact that they continue to change their mind about what the Bible says, means they are not the inerrant Word of God, and there is likely another underlying motivation!

As I continued to weigh the truth of the belief system and the cost for speaking up in any way against it, I also had to look at the outcomes or the results that have come from the belief system. Obviously, my results didn't always play out well. But I have also seen the outcome in the children in the circles I'm in and can see that many of them are no longer believers of Jesus. In hearing them say why they don't believe any longer, they say that it is because of "hypocrisy" of the church saying one thing and doing another. But they also describe experiences that were taught as the truth but are inconsistent with God's Word. And then I weigh the behaviors with what the Holy Spirit is showing me and whether there is manipulation or twisting of the situation that has the red flags you would see when the enemy is involved. What I can say is this. We each have to take this same exercise and weigh it yourself and decide based on your experience. For me and my family, we weighed everything and decided that we felt called to move forward in churches that honor and support women in leadership, including in pastoral positions.

Let's take this one step further. There was a point in my journey, around 2019, when I was becoming more aware of the Holy Spirit, that I also became aware of demonic strategies that were being used to stop ministries and churches from moving into what God was calling them to. I started to see patterns of behavior in varying situations that seemed to be more than coincidence. And then God began to use my gift of discernment to begin to discern spirits. Discerning what people are doing in this world by worldly sight and experience is very different than discerning when there is a spirit behind the behavior. One of the first encounters I had was with someone who was admittedly operating in witchcraft.

I was at a worship night and a young lady began to stare at me in a way that was out of the norm. I knew fairly quickly that something was different in the spirit and can only describe it as she was trying to get me to pay attention to her. I asked the Holy Spirit what to do and He said to love her from afar. I did talk to her several times, each time a different personality including a child manifesting, while also praying for her. I somehow knew that she was trying to block our prayers and our worship of Jesus, so I began instinctually interceding to break her efforts to stop the worshipers. That night she and some friends of hers followed the worship leaders to a restaurant they went to and showed up at their table at the restaurant proclaiming the coincidence. The problem was these coincidences and other odd circumstances kept happening until the minds of the worship leaders were tormented and the worship nights stopped. I have witnessed this same type of scenario happen to prayer groups and ministry groups many times and have also watched this same person, outwardly and admittedly operating in witchcraft, go from church to church with worship and prayer groups ending in similar ways following her involvement. And I have also now watched her become more powerful as she has built a team of friends who prey on unsuspecting churches and the kindness of believers. Less than four years ago I would have told you that you were crazy for saying these things. But today, I can see it becoming pervasive in our communities, through the gift of discerning of spirits.

We know from Luke 10:19, that Jesus said, "I have given you authority to trample on snakes and scorpions and to overcome all the power of the enemy; nothing will harm you." And as we have discussed, there are many Scriptures that warn of the enemy and what he is allowed to do on earth and there are many more that talk about demonic spirits, principalities, and powers. If you are like me though, attending more conservative churches, you may have no understanding or even believe that any of these things can still happen today, except to have been told it's against the rules. But there came a point in my journey when I began to transition my thoughts and understanding from an earthly understanding to a spiritual one. When someone tells you they are practicing witchcraft or are a witch, you should believe them! Would you ever say that if you weren't? And you should be very careful how you proceed. We have authority over all of it but if you are unaware of how it operates you can be played for a while and lulled into the behaviors that go along with it.

What I've now experienced multiple times is that while a person operating in witchcraft is partnered with the demonic, they don't look like the devil, and you won't see the evil side of them until they get entangled with you and your circle of friends. They will initially present to you seemingly innocent, with things like crystals, tarot cards and fairies for example. But then they will slowly introduce more invasive strategies like using scripture to say your loved one wants to speak to you from the dead or predicting your future relationships or career moves. That is how they get into your circle. When you ask them who they worship, the person will often say Jesus, but the spirit behind it will not say Jesus' name. So how do you know the difference? First, Scripture tells you what to do and what not to do, specifically to present Jesus to the spirit and they will flee, and I've see them do exactly that. Spells, incantations, circles of witches displayed in yards as part of the décor, the third eye that is on everything now including jewelry, movies, and television shows where people are agreeing with and stating they are witches, it all matters. But second, the Holy Spirit will guide you. I now understand another outcome from not having a relationship with the Holy Spirit, is that you are a prime target for witchcraft, and other spiritual attacks for that matter, because your belief system won't alert you to the possibility at all. I'll let you look more into this on your own and again, there are resources in the back of the book you can look at regarding these things. But just know it's real and your participation in it matters to God and it's another door you can open to sin. And God's purpose in revealing it to me, was to give me some wisdom I didn't have and to develop some tools in me to see what was trying to destroy my peace and the ministry.

You and I are saved and covered by all authority in heaven and the enemy cannot prevail against us or God's plans. However, there is definitely more going on in the church and the world today than just bad behavior. And, if you're like me, and you were raised to snub our noses at anything regarding the devil, I learned the hard way, that he can and does disrupt our lives and will use the smallest sin to foster bigger and bigger agreement to do some really mean-spirited things in the name of Jesus. And we all need to be better at discerning these types of things, and then respond to them with the tools and authority Jesus gave us to respond.

Reflection

1. Do you see signs of witchcraft in your town? What specifically? Why do you think God allows you to see it when others can't?
2. Have you ever researched the symbols on your town's government buildings? What did you find?
3. How do you discern and respond to bad behavior?
4. How does God speak to or alert you to, the things going on around you?
5. Can you see or feel evil when it is present? What signs does your body give you?

CHAPTER 8

THE POWER OF HER SPIRITUAL GIFTS

"There are different kinds of gifts, but the same Spirit distributes them. There are different kinds of service, but the same Lord. There are different kinds of working, but in all of them and in everyone it is the same God at work. Now to each one the manifestation of the Spirit is given for the common good."

—I CORINTHIANS 12:4-7

The power of your spiritual gifts is first to understand that they are gifts to help you overcome the world and help build up others. They're not just a list of attributes to achieve nor are they a thing of past biblical culture to be ignored. They are exactly what they say they are; gifts and spiritual meaning they cannot be gained for some nefarious purpose, and you have to have a relationship with the Holy Spirit to work through how to use them for God's purposes in your own calling and purpose. And, because context is so important in understanding Scripture, the verses surrounding these gifts, are grounded in love, a sincere desire to see others made whole and loved by God.

As a former business owner and leader and now a college professor who teaches leadership and entrepreneurship, I have been helping people discover their strengths, spiritual gifts, personality traits, love languages, etc. for years. And while those things are all effective tools in business and even church environments to help determine the best positions for employees, they never fully hit the target spiritually. They've never connected me to God and how He designed me. But during this journey, when God led me to read about the spiritual gifts known as the fivefold ministry, for the first time in my life I finally intimately understood myself and the way that I'm wired. And I began to see how these foundational functions were part of the key that was missing in understanding my ministry season and why I didn't fit in.

You should know that *fivefold* is not a term you will find in the Bible but instead a man-made term used to describe the five spiritual gifts of apostle, prophet, evangelist, pastor, and teacher. Following our departure from our former church and a move to a new church in 2019, I met with the new pastor and shared some of our prior limiting experiences and asked him where I should start in rebuilding. He suggested I take a fivefold ministry assessment and shared a link where I could do that, and I did. The results of the assessment and the description that came back described the way that I had operated my entire life in detail. Much of what it said about me were things that no one could ever have known because it included the way that I think and interact with people and some of the embarrassing ways that I get stuck over and over again. But it was more than that: it felt like the report described part of my DNA. I now believed I had all of the puzzle pieces for restoring my identity, but God also began to show me that it wasn't just about my own identity but that He also needed to help me discover my own unique purpose and that the spiritual gifts were foundational to that pursuit. The fivefold ministry gifts and how they function can be seen in Scripture, starting with Ephesians 4:11–16:

So Christ himself gave the apostles, the prophets, the evangelists, the pastors, and teachers, to equip his people for works of service, so that the body of Christ may be built up until we all reach unity in the faith and in the knowledge of the Son of God and become mature, attaining to the whole measure of the fullness of Christ. Then we will no longer be infants, tossed back and forth by the waves, and blown here and there by every wind of teaching and by the cunning and craftiness of people in their deceitful scheming. Instead, speaking the truth in love, we will grow to become in every respect the mature body of him who is the head, that is, Christ. From him the whole body, joined and held together by every supporting ligament, grows, and builds itself up in love, as each part does its work.

Further, in 1 Corinthians 12:20–31, we see a description of the body of Christ:

As it is, there are many parts, but one body. The eye cannot say to the hand, "I don't need you!" And the head cannot say to the feet, "I don't need you!" On the contrary, those parts of the body that seem to be weaker are indispensable, and the parts that we think are less honorable we treat with special honor. And the parts that are unpresentable are treated with special modesty, while our presentable parts need no special treatment. But God has put the body together, giving greater honor to the parts that lacked it, so that there should be no division in the body, but that its parts should have equal concern for each other. If one part suffers, every part suffers with it; if one part is honored, every part rejoices with it. Now you are the body of Christ, and each one of you is a part of it. And God has placed in the church first of all apostles, second prophets, third teachers, then miracles, then gifts of healing, of helping, of guidance, and of different kinds of tongues. Are all apostles? Are all prophets? Are all teachers? Do all work miracles? Do all have gifts of healing? Do all speak in tongues? Do all interpret? Now eagerly desire the greater gifts.

To summarize, the fivefold gifts referred to in Ephesians were given by Jesus himself to equip the body of Christ for works of service so that we can reach unity in faith and knowledge of Jesus and become mature and not be taken down by the enemy. In this way, the whole body can grow and build itself up in love as each part does its work. According to 1 Corinthians, God gave certain gifts to the church in order so that the body of Christ could operate together, having equal concern for others, sharing in each other's suffering and rejoicing. People have written many books on each of these gifts and the interpretation of these scriptures; feel free to research and spend as much time as you need to on these analyses. But you should study the scriptures for yourself. I've listed some resources in the back of the book to help with this. For the purposes of this chapter, though, I want to introduce you to these fivefold gift definitions and try to move you into a place of peace about who you are and how God designed you! Also, as a point of clarification, there are many interpretations around the fivefold gifts and even some denominations that point to them as positions and titles versus gifts. The focus of this exercise is to look at them as spiritual gifts that help the church function as the body of Christ. That's it.

Apostles know, feel, and hear from God as their primary way of communication. They can see the "gold" in people, recognizing how God designed them, and also God's plans for their future. They know what God is doing and who should be in what position. The word *apostle* literally means to be sent from one place to another to establish culture and was a secular term before it was used by Jesus to describe people who were sent into a newly conquered territory to establish the culture of the conquering government.[9] Apostles are messengers of God who are sent forth to transform culture with the good news. Many people operating in this gift end up feeling rejected by the church because they don't realize that others can't see what they see or know. And even when they try to explain what they see or know, if they are unaware of God's Word and are not operating in the Holy Spirit, they will not be able to explain it themselves yet. The apostle comes first in order according to the Scripture, which means God uses the apostolic gift to start things and those with the gift are often drawn to and placed in leadership positions. This makes sense in that God will want to impart His vision first to someone who can receive it and write the plans with Him first before anyone can build and sustain the plan! The apostle has a function similar to that of a founder or CEO in business and thinks in terms of God's plans, solutions, and experiences, wanting to empower the body of Christ. When you present a problem to someone with apostolic gifting, their first response will be, "Let's do something about it."

Prophets reveal God's heart to His people, giving guidance to individuals and the body, also sharing revelation as well as interpretation, application, and timing. The prophet also hears and sees from God and is meant to be partnered with the apostle, helping to validate and execute the vision God has given the apostle. But the prophet adds the ability to discern and interpret the times and seasons to help guide the apostle when it is time to execute the vision. Prophets help launch those people who have been identified into a particular ministry calling and assignment. The prophet hears from God and is often a seer into the heavenly realm and speaks in a way that I call the language of heaven, which when you hear it, you know it came from God. Prophets often spend their childhood seeing angels or even

demons and being afraid of what they were experiencing, not knowing what to do with their experiences. Many prophets I have talked
to also remember asking God to remove those things in their youth,
not realizing they are part of their gifting. As a point of distinction,
prophets and the gift of prophecy are two different gifts. We'll cover
the gift of prophecy later in the chapter, but they are often confused
with each other. Prophet's function like the chief innovation officer,
or CIO, in business but think in terms of spirituality, not achievement.

An evangelist desires everyone to be part of the kingdom of God
and is anointed to preach the gospel and point people to Jesus while
inviting them into the church. They will often operate in the supernatural gifts that help to confirm their message. Evangelist's recruit and
encourage people to accept their position in God's vision and mission
and then celebrate the testimonies. If you've ever met the charismatic
person whom everyone likes to emulate or follow, you've likely met
someone operating in the evangelist grace. They can sell anything
but especially like selling things that are of God. You'll know them
by their networks, their infectious smiles, and their desire to bring
people together. Evangelists blow things up in a good way! They take
what has been built by the apostles and prophets and take it to the
next level. They create a tipping point for success and for a movement.
And they love to share the gospel in big ways, like on stages and at
conferences. They are likely involved in revival movements and church
activities wherever they go. They can't help themselves! Evangelists
create converts, while apostles create disciples. The evangelist is similar
to the salesperson in business but always thinks in terms of God's
goodness, So they have to believe in what they are selling.

Pastors are literally the heart of the Church, gifted to take care of
the body of Christ. And I don't mean that they are necessarily the
positional person in the church; I'm talking about how they are hardwired to think and operate. Any person with any of these gifts could
be a pastor by title in a church; each would just operate differently.
The pastoral gift exudes love for people and the ability to include

and connect people, listen, and counsel people, and if they are fully operating in their gifting, they will facilitate supernatural healing and restoration in people. The pastor is often a "feeler" and will have a hard time with and not understand the apostle who is driven more by vision and mission, but the pastor will keep loving them anyway! Many pastoral-led churches are accused of "sweeping things under the rug." I would argue that it's because a pastoral-led church and a pastor operating in his or her gifting will have a hard time drawing a line around a negative event or even criminal behavior because the foundation of how they were designed is to offer grace, forgiveness, and reconciliation. Part of the reason we are missing the mark in many churches today is that many churches are operating in the pastoral gift and fear healthy conflict, seeing it as not being "kind", and they are operating alone without the other ministry gifts to help them in the area's they are not gifted. The pastor is similar to the human resources officer in business and thinks in terms of relationships.

Teachers teach and edify the church, protecting and defending the Bible and helping make complex things simple for others so they can apply it to their lives. Teachers also teach others in the body of Christ to learn and discover the Bible and how to apply it to their lives. Teachers understand and explain God's truth and wisdom. They help the body of Christ remain biblically grounded and train God's people how to live in the kingdom of God. Teachers also contain profound insight and help believers see dynamics in the kingdom of God they have never seen before. They will remember details and can quickly point to a scripture or conflicting scriptures from different books or chapters of the Bible. And teachers also help us to know the Word so that we cannot be deceived by the enemy through twisted scripture. The teacher is similar to the chief training officer, or CTO, in business and thinks in terms of knowledge.

There are combinations of these gifts that work together better and others that have an inherent tension in them. The differences are meant to complement the body of Christ, but when they instead become competing influences in an environment of religion that requires power and control, they can clash. For example, while prophets reveal the heart of God, teachers reveal His mind. Prophets have revelations of hidden things in the future, while teachers can be rigid in interpretation. Teachers reveal the specifics of God's truth, while prophets reveal from other lenses or perspectives. Teachers are lifelong learners' content with where they are, while prophets are interpreting the times and looking to the future. Apostles, on the other hand, are called to start and build things, but when they are finished, God often calls them out to build the next thing. This can be especially troubling for apostles who don't understand that they aren't supposed to hang on to the thing they just built, which is similar to how a business founder would feel walking away from the company they built. But it's also troubling because when it's time for the apostle to move on, not only do they hear from God to move but the prophet, evangelist, pastor, and teacher also hear it from God, and their encouragement or exhortation from those team members that they also believe the leader should move on can feel like rejection. Additionally, if the team isn't mature in their training in the fivefold to understand that apostles are often called by God to move on as a positive move, they will dismiss the apostle too soon or altogether and expect them to move on as an act of wrongdoing rather than honor.

In churches, often apostles and prophets start and build a church, much like you would in business, and then once it is running for a while and board members and elders are added to the vision, there is a move to dismiss the founders. Some of this is because the apostles and prophets are always going to move forward and change things when God says change. It is how they are wired. But pastors and teachers who become the leaders in churches, are not wired for change, they are wired to stay set and keep the status quo. The best example of this is seen in denominations who replace the pastor regularly with a new "teacher" to carry on the legacy. Then when God is ready to shift the church, there are no apostolic and prophetic leaders to lead the change.

To give you an example of how these gifts work, my husband is gifted as a teacher, and I am gifted as an apostle/prophet. When we have a discussion or even an argument, I always start my understanding of the topic from a big-picture perspective and move into the details. For me the point of the discussion is always, "How do I solve this problem or complete the plan?" Conversely, he starts his points in the details, using his knowledge of things I would never spend time memorizing unless I was engaged in a project around it. We often laugh, sometimes with frustration, when we realize we are saying the same thing as we both finally get to the point. We also tend to complete the discussion with what the other one doesn't see or understand. When I need to understand the way, something outside of the project I'm working on works in detail, he always knows those answers. I can then use his detail of other things, to help put words or plans to something I'm working on and combine them with what God has given me. For example, as God was re-teaching me His Word in 2020, he told me that His plans were designed in an "ecosystem" approach not a hierarchical approach. I knew what an ecosystem was in my mind and understanding, but I couldn't put words to it in the world. I somehow instinctually knew what God meant by it, but I didn't know how to explain it to others. So I asked my husband to define it from a science perspective which helped me describe it to others. (We will discuss ecosystems in a future chapter.)

In addition to the gifts separated out and labeled the fivefold gifts, which are generally recognized as the ministry gifts, there are many spiritual gifts listed in Scripture. All of the gifts are available to all believers, and you may or may not operate in each of them over a lifetime. They can also come and go, but they are yours to seek out and use for the purpose of building up the body of Christ and some help persuade unbelievers. If you're like me, you may have taken an assessment and discovered some of these spiritual gifts, but have they ever been tangible in your life? Did you ever go after them? The spiritual gifts are separated different ways depending on the purpose. For simplicity, I'm going to divide the gifts by ministry gifts which we have already discussed and were left to us by Jesus, motivational gifts which are given to us by God at birth, and manifestation gifts which are gifts given to us by the Holy Spirit.

The motivational gifts are found in Romans 12:3–8 says, "For by the grace given me I say to every one of you: Do not think of yourself more highly than you ought, but rather think of yourself with sober judgment, in accordance with the faith God has distributed to each of you. For just as each of us has one body with many members, and these members do not all have the same function, so in Christ we, though many, form one body, and each member belongs to all the others. We have different gifts, according to the grace given to each of us. If your gift is prophesying, then prophesy in accordance with your faith; if it is serving, then serve; if it is teaching, then teach; if it is to encourage, then give encouragement; if it is giving, then give generously; if it is to lead, do it diligently; if it is to show mercy, do it cheerfully." A few other gifts are mentioned in different places in Scripture as well. In Romans 15:5 we find the gift of the spirit of unity, the ability to see the giftings in others as different but interdependent. In 1 Corinthians 12:28 is the gift to rule or govern and execute plans, called the gift of administration. And in Ephesians 1:17 Paul mentions the ability to hear from God and have Him reveal Scripture in a way others have never heard before.

The manifestation gifts are found in 1 Corinthians 12:4-11 and are given to us by God at salvation. The following list will help you pursue each of them through the reading of the Word and having the Holy Spirit allow you to see this gift in yourself. Again, these gifts are all attainable and the Holy Spirit guides you in becoming wise in them. I Corinthians 12:4–11 says,

There are different kinds of gifts, but the same Spirit distributes them. There are different kinds of service, but the same Lord. There are different kinds of working, but in all of them and in everyone it is the same God at work. Now to each one the manifestation of the Spirit is given for the common good. To one there is given through the Spirit a message of wisdom, to another a message of knowledge by means of the same Spirit, to another faith by the same Spirit, to another gifts of healing by that one Spirit, to another miraculous powers, to another prophecy, to another distinguishing between spirits, to another speaking in different kinds of tongues, and to still another the interpretation of tongues. All these are the work of one and the same Spirit, and he distributes them to each one, just as he determines.

To briefly summarize how each of these gifts is defined, prophecy means to declare the will, purposes, and truth of God. Serving means to minister to or provide service to others. Encouraging means to build others up, strengthen their faith, and comfort them during trials, giving of your money, time, or talents. Leadership influences others by guiding them with wisdom and grace. Mercy is showing empathy and compassion to others. Lastly, the manifestation gifts are, wisdom which is speaking biblical truths to others with discernment. The gift of knowledge refers to speaking something no one else could know to build up faith. Faith is confidence in God and His promise, truths, and Word. Healing is the ability to partner with God and bring supernatural healing to others. Distinguishing between spirits is being able to discern when demonic spirits are at play in a situation. Speaking in tongues involves speaking in languages unknown to others except to those who are supposed to hear. Interpretation of tongues is the gift to interpret the tongues.

Your unique combination of spiritual gifts are a significant part of what makes your identity and purpose different from everyone else's around you, and it is also consistent with how God wired you. So, if you've allowed something to change who you are, or have settled into a position or place in life that is inconsistent with your gifting, you will eventually get burned out. Conversely, when you are operating in your authentic identity and purpose, you will walk in freedom and joy, bringing you energy to do the work. Identity disruption is when someone or something takes away from who you were supposed to be. When we realize that our identity and purpose are God's gifts to us and we find them, our lives and life decisions will bring us peace in who we are and relentless passion in what we do. Last, these gifts and especially the fivefold leadership functions, are meant to give us distinction in the body of Christ, but also help us understand ow to work together in teams.

We will continue to dive deeper into these gifts in future chapters, but for not know that when you are trying to operate outside of your gifts, unless God calls you and anoints you to, you will feel it, often as a burden rather than a gift. God equips us with everything we need to protect and defend ourselves and others from the schemes of the enemy, but if we don't even understand that we have authority in them, then we become sitting ducks for his plans. Jesus gives us all authority, women too, in a variety of areas. If you're like me, you may believe that authority is reserved for men only, but that is not what Scripture says.

Reflection

1. What does identity mean to you?
2. Have you ever considered what purposes God designed uniquely for you?
3. What fivefold gift do you most resonate with?
4. What past behaviors can you identify that seem to be explained better now that you understand the fivefold gifts better?
5. What spiritual gifts are you already experienced in? Are there others you would like to have?

CHAPTER 9

THE POWER OF HER AUTHORITY

"For dominion belongs to the Lord and he rules over the nations."

—PSALM 22:28

The real power of your authority is Jesus and is recognized when you are equipped in God's truth, in partnership with the Holy Spirit, while discerning, defending, and breaking what the enemy intends for bad. This is the type of authority you have when dealing with spiritual warfare. But a second type of authority is spoken about in the Bible and that is the authority of every believer to represent Jesus, called the priesthood of all believers. Authority is defined by websters dictionary as the power to influence or command thought, opinion, or behavior, a person in command or a convincing force.[10] If you're a believer, you're authority comes from God, not from man. And though being in community with other believers and having others who guide us and mentor us in spiritual authority is good, ultimately God is the one who calls us to His work and places us in position to fulfill His purposes on earth. A third type of authority spoken about in Scripture is governing authority, both in the context of trusting God with whom He chooses to govern in the world, but governing authority in the Church. While each of these three types of authority are important and have their own purposes, most of the limiting beliefs are grounded in the authority to govern.

At the beginning of 2017 in the time I have described as a transition out of ministry, God was very clear with me that it was time to *shut it down*. I now know it's because He had shown me and tested me enough to be able to mold me into who He called me to be and do. Though it took the next five years to officially shut down the ministry from a legal standpoint, from 2018 to 2021 was the worst time of my life and incredibly difficult. I now understand that because of my own immaturity in a few things, I had unknowingly partnered with the enemy to create a toxic environment for both me and those around me in the ministry and in my businesses. First, from a positive standpoint, I desired greatly to see men and women work together, but I didn't know how to discern when, how and who to bring into the mission. Second, I was a people pleaser and cared way too much for my own good what people thought of me. And third, I had no training, as I've mentioned, on how to do ministry and handle the environment. Prior to the ministry season, I was described in business as kind-hearted but unwavering in my convictions, and fair. But following my season in ministry, I had allowed the enemy's strategies and the behaviors associated with them, to take me down completely, silence my voice, lose my confidence, and strip me of hope. How did this happen? If you were to try and explain it in a worldly way, you would have to conclude that I was a horrible person, leader, and a complete failure in ministry. And trust me, I did that for myself, as

I listened to the gossip, accusations and whispers of the enemy and others who were partnering with his strategies too. But that is not what God intended for me and in order to restore me, I had to go through the painful process of reconciling all of these things. And authority had a lot to do with the reasons that I found myself where I was, when I met God in the shower in 2021.

First, I had partnered with and intertwined the ministry and my business endeavors, with the church and the limiting belief systems operating in the spirit of religion. I applied the church's limiting belief system to everything I was doing. Second, I partnered with and intertwined the ministry and my businesses with the Ahab and Jezebel spirits by tolerating those behaviors from the people around me. Third, I partnered with and intertwined the ministry and my businesses with the spirit of politics by setting us in position to receive grants from the government and getting sucked into what I now know was a very manipulative, controlling and sometimes corrupt system. Fourth, I partnered with and intertwined the ministry and my businesses with the spirit of fraternity and my passion to see men and women working together and found myself on the outside look-ing into my own companies and watching them be taken by people I trusted. And finally, I allowed the spirit of leviathan to twist all of us to the point where we all walked away, mad at each other, feeling dazed and confused by what had just happened. And I led the effort. I wanted the authority, but I wasn't equipped spiritually to yield my sword in a mature way yet. Of course God knew that which is the point of being refined in His fire, but I didn't understand it yet. I did understand though instinctually, that when God said shut it down and it took five years to unwind the mess I had made, that it was what I had to do if I wanted to see any fruit in ministry moving forward.

The truth is authority comes from God and while it brings the power to influence others, if it comes only through position recognized by the world, the outcomes, and the way it's measured is culture's outcome and will not fulfill the yearning inside of you to find your divine identity and purpose. In hindsight, I was called by God, but the church didn't confirm the call and the way that I tried to lead it was worldly instead of with the anointing and spiritual leadership skills that I now understand God was building in me through the process. So, now what? I'm on the other side of this now, but at the time, I did not believe I would get a second chance. I had lost everything and was stripped of all of it at the same time. The next step to restoring me, was for God to help me see the truth about my season through the Scripture and how and who He places in authority.

First, as a reminder from the prior chapters on discernment and warfare, we have authority in Luke 10:19, to "trample on snakes and scorpions and to overcome all the power of the enemy". And in Genesis 1:25 we are given authority to rule over mankind. "Let us make mankind in our image, in our likeness, so that they may rule over the fish in the sea and the birds in the sky, over the livestock and all the wild animals, and over all the creatures that move along the ground." Second, in 1 Peter 2:9 we read about the authority God has given us as believers to represent Jesus: "But you are a chosen people, a royal priesthood, a holy nation, God's special possession, that you may declare the praises of him who called you out of darkness into his wonderful light." God designed us all to be His priests and have authority on earth and in heaven, including over Satan and his schemes. With the help of the Holy Spirit, as we've discussed, the more you begin to depend on Him daily for understanding in all things, especially when they don't seem right, the more you will be guided to see, hear, feel, and know what is happening around you from a spiritual perspective. And we all have the authority and are commissioned by Jesus in Matthew 28:16-20 to share the gospel and make disciples, "Then the eleven disciples went to Galilee, to the mountain where Jesus had told them to go. When they saw him, they worshiped him; but some doubted. Then Jesus came to them and said, "All authority in heaven and on earth has been given to me. Therefore go and make disciples of all nations, baptizing them in the name of the Father and of the Son and of the Holy Spirit, and teaching them to obey everything I have commanded you. And surely, I am with you always, to the very end of the age."

One area of contention for women, including me, in the area of authority is that the limiting belief system in conservative churches was the unwillingness to recognize that a woman could be called, ordained, or commissioned. If you can't be a pastor, you can't be called by God for His purposes, therefore you can't be commissioned. And since you can't be called or commissioned, you don't need discipleship or mentoring. Though I no longer believe that this is what Scripture says, and that Jesus is who ultimately commissions us, if the church you are in does not believe this, then the right thing to do is confirm the belief system at that particular church and do what God says to do. There are many examples of women who were commissioned and led and were called. In mine and my family's situation. God did not call us to leave the church until He had allowed us to confirm the belief system and go on good terms. Despite this, when we left, we were removed from all communication and our departure after fifteen years of service was not shared with the church, leaving all of the people we thought we were friends with, wondering what awful thing happened for us to leave. And while we have many good memories of our time there, it was no longer where God wanted us to be and in order for us to move into our next ministry calling, He would need to move us to do so, and our obedience had a cost to it.

In hindsight, I also now understand that God did commission me to start the nonprofit ministry Himself and He arranged for close to one-hundred people in that church to confirm it and lay hands on my husband and I as we began that call. Commissioning is defined by Merriam-Webster as a formal written warrant granting the power to perform various acts or duties, an authorization, or a command to act in a prescribed manner or to perform prescribed acts, or a task or matter entrusted to one as an agent for another. And in Matthew 28:19, we are all commissioned to go and make disciples and baptize people. But we are also cautioned to respect and not rebel against authority. In Romans 13:1, "Let everyone be subject to the governing authorities, for there is no authority except that which God has established. The authorities that exist have been established by God." And in 1 Timothy 2:1-2 were asked to pray for those in authority, "I urge, then, first of all, that petitions, prayers, intercession and thanksgiving be made for all people — for kings and all those in authority, that we may live peaceful and quiet lives in all godliness and holiness." Ultimately though, authority belongs to God, Psalm 22:28, "for dominion belongs to the Lord and he rules over the nations".

But where authority starts and stops, and in what situations it is Scriptural and what areas it is not, is one of the most twisted areas of the Bible that is used by the enemy to control and manipulate believers, especially women. And because the enemy often knows Scripture better than those of us who believe and follow Jesus, we unknowingly partner with lies that God never intended. The version of the Bible also matters and changes depending on who did the interpretation. So, as much as I would like to avoid this section of the book, because these were things God revealed to me and corrected my thinking on, I'm also going to pass them on to you. Here are a few tips God taught me. First, remember I said I had a deal with Him that He would always show me things three times. Often, He would reveal something to me in a dream or vision that most of the time I had zero knowledge of or know that it was in the Bible. Then He would take me through Scripture using multiple versions of the Bible and then He would confirm it through another minister or teacher. And finally, He would reconcile it for me, just like He did when I discerned lies as a special investigator, and He would highlight evidence to me.

To have any legitimate discussion about authority, you also have to have to understand submission and what it means to be submissive. If you're like me, and that word was used to control you, it is not a word that brings joy. But let's try and see how God intended it to be interpreted. Submission is defined by Websters dictionary, as a legal agreement or the act of submitting to authority, while being submissive means to humble yourself or be compliant. In the Bible though, when the Scripture talks about submission it is the act of putting God's desires before your own and bearing with each other.

Submission is empowering and grounded in love resulting in peace and harmony. Oppression is grounded in control and results in division and oppression.

Now with lens of empowerment and love resulting in peace and harmony in mind, read the following verses in Scripture that discuss authority and submission. In Hebrews 13:17, "Have confidence in your leaders and submit to their authority, because they keep watch over you as those who must give an account. Do this so that their work will be a joy, not a burden, for that would be of no benefit to you." This means to be agreeable and to work together with each other. It does not mean you cannot ask question and be peers with each other and sometimes need to work out your differences

In Ephesians 5:21-28, "Submit to one another out of reverence for Christ. Wives, submit yourselves to your own husbands as you do to the Lord. For the husband is the head of the wife as Christ is the head of the church, his body, of which he is the Savior. Now as the church submits to Christ, so also wives should submit to their husbands in everything. Husbands, love your wives, just as Christ loved the church and gave himself up for her to make her holy, cleansing her by the washing with water through the word, and to present her to himself as a radiant church, without stain or wrinkle or any other blemish, but holy and blameless. In this same way, husbands ought to love their wives as their own bodies. He who loves his wife loves himself." Again, the meaning of this scripture is intended through the lens of love and empowerment, bearing with each other, and working through your differences. It does not man control and oppression.

So, to recap. God is the ultimate authority. He gives us our anointing and position, but He also allows us to go through testing and failure in order to equip us to be who and what He has designed us to be and do. And he intends for the church to lay hands on us and approve our position and calling. But for women, when many in the church refuse this step, you may have to rely on your relationship with the Holy Spirit and God to know what the right thing to do is. And finally, the Scriptures are specific. We are all equipped and called and given authority to trample the enemy. And we are all called and commissioned to share Jesus and preach the gospel. But Scripture can be interpreted to say that Jesus only ordained men to govern the church. I no longer believe this interpretation personally but if you do, it's not wrong, unless it negates what God is asking you to do

Reflection

1. Has God ever said "yes" to your calling and the church said "no"? How did you handle it?
2. What areas of authority has God called you to?
3. What areas of your life did you give up on believing you could not be called to those areas?
4. Is there anything you would do different now?
5. If submission is still a word that triggers a negative response, ask the Holy Spirit where to start in healing that part of your identity and purpose.

CHAPTER 10

THE POWER OF HER INCUBATED PURPOSE

"Many are the plans in a person's heart, but it is the Lord's purpose that prevails."

—PROVERBS 19:21

The power of your Purpose is being empowered by the Holy Spirit as He prophesies and incubates your passions into existence. The Holy Spirit gives you a burning in your belly that you cannot get rid of until you do something about it. The way that He prepares you for that purpose is to equip you to understand spiritual warfare, discernment, your spiritual gifts, and your authority. Each of these things are hopefully clearer after reading the previous chapters, than they were before you started. To incubate means[11], "to sit on (eggs) so as to hatch by the warmth of the body, to maintain (something, such as an embryo or a chemically active system) under conditions favorable for hatching, development, or reaction, or to cause or aid the development of, to support your growth". In the Bible we see the word "brood" which means to hatch, to conceive or to plan. When God places you in an incubator season, he is prophesying over you your purpose and preparing you for it. He not only protects you, but he sustains you through it. God develops us into His image through the pressure and testing of life's circumstances as He uses temptation to expose our weaknesses. The key is not to lose your identity (who you are) while walking out your purpose (what you do). This distinction of who you are verses what you do will continue to be a theme as we move forward. For many men, their purpose is who they are, but for most women, that is not how we define ourselves, Remember, most men lead through achievement and most women lead through responsibility. That's a huge distinction.

Purpose is defined as your "why", what desire is in you that is outside of yourself. If you're a believer the originator of that passion is God. But God's purposes are different than those in this world. Of course He gives us purpose on earth, and He wants us to be refined into a calling that is in alignment with His Kingdom purposes and will during different times and seasons. But we all seem to have an innate desire towards purpose. As a believer, as you continue to pursue Him, He will also place in you a desire to understand your place in God's Kingdom. Ultimately, this is what many define as *calling*, as I did when I jumped into ministry. But it is more than that. It is belonging and being a part of something bigger than yourself which is why when it is disrupted it feels like rejection. So, as you move into the next component of your ultimate calling, Leadership, and you find yourself being refined by fire, a season that is often when many of the things you have been building will be taken, you will want to be careful not to respond to the season by letting things stop you instead of propelling you. The first step of calling is reconciling everything that has happened in your refinement season, and many of the things that have happened in your lifetime as well.

Your purpose is what you do but it is also a reflection of who you are. Your purpose will becomes defined during your warfare season and as you begin to discover your spiritual gifts. In my experience, when people talk about their purpose, they usually get emotional about it and while it might take some work to discover what exactly it is, as God incubates you in your season of discovering and establishing your purpose, you will know it when you get there. As you continue to work through the PINK framework and the book, begin to consider what your fivefold ministry gifting might be. Destinyfinder.com is a great resource for a comprehensive fivefold assessment. I have also included some questions that I have used over the years to help point people in the right direction in the back of the book.[12]

In the next section of the PINK Framework, God began to allow me to take on leadership roles in my area of *calling*, while He tested me and refined me into Kingdom thinking, instead of worldly thinking. Healthy leaders have one thing in common that is rarely talked about in public leadership circles: an encounter with God and a season in the refining fire. Leaders can lead without having been tested or going through the fire, but Kingdom Leadership is evidenced by restoration, an encounter with God, a mantle and anointing in your area of calling; creativity, freedom, and innovation; and ultimately the refinement of our voice and your message. When you meet someone who has gone through these things, you will know it. And when you get to the end of it and still have a driving passion that you can't let go of, God has now tested and refined your motivations and your heart posture to keep going.

Reflection

1. What areas of your life has God been highlighting to you that you can't let go of?
2. What are your spiritual gifts? If you don't know, there are assessments you can take to find out. But for now based on the definitions what ones do you resonate with?
3. Have you ever suffered an illness the doctors could not explain? How did experienced healing from it?
4. Have you ever experienced spiritual warfare? What experiences can you now look back on and reconcile whether man, God or the devil were the authors of?
5. What will you do differently now that you know that sin can open up a partnership with the enemy?

CHAPTER 11

THE POWER
OF HER
RESTORATION

"It is for freedom that Christ has set us free.
Stand firm, then, and do not let yourselves be
burdened again by a yoke of slavery."

—GALATIANS 5:1

The power of restoration is the ability to reconcile what has been broken, either between you and God or between you and man and be able to move forward in, and sustain, freedom with a different perspective. The first step of restoration is to acknowledge the truth and to create awareness around the truth so that you can come into agreement with God on how to move forward. The key is to restore your relationship with God first, and then to listen to His instruction for restoring relationships with others. Recognize though that as God begins to restore you, He's going to ask you to let go of some of the people and things, maybe even most things from the past. Hopefully, the content in previous chapters has helped you to reconcile with God and see for yourself that He is not the one perpetuating the limiting beliefs or condoning bad behavior.

The second step, then, is to reconcile with others who were part of your journey and try to find a place of agreement that can include agreeing to disagree. The Church is always going to have different expressions, and having the belief that only men, for example, can be senior pastors, is likely not a battle God will have you or me fight because Scripture can be interpreted that way. Having said that, it is almost impossible to have that belief system and honor women in every other way without bias. He *will* have us fight the behaviors that go along with that limiting belief about women's roles and the attempt to extend that belief to culture. The good news is that He *will* tell you where to go and how to handle every situation. And He will never ask you to do something that is against His Word.

In Matthew 18:15-20 we see, "If your brother or sister sins, go and point out their fault, just between the two of you. If they listen to you, you have won them over. But if they will not listen, take one or two others along, so that 'every matter may be established by the testimony of two or three witnesses. If they still refuse to listen, tell it to the church; and if they refuse to listen even to the church, treat them as you would a pagan or a tax collector. Truly I tell you, whatever you bind on earth will be bound in heaven, and whatever you loose on earth will be loosed in heaven. Again, truly I tell you that if two of you on earth agree about anything they ask for, it will be done for them by my Father in heaven. For where two or three gather in my name, there am I with them." This verse references a path for church members to go to a person privately to work out a sin against them, and then take it to more people making it more public, in the hope that apologies and forgiveness can be secured. We have authority to bind (tie up) and loose (free) sin on Jesus' behalf. And the next verse, quoted often in by itself, says that when two or more of you can come to agreement, anything you ask for will be done for them by our Father in Heaven.

In reconciling abusive behaviors in culture, the response is similar to that recommended above in the Church, except that there are now laws against these behaviors and prescribed recourse. Unfortunately, the law seldom resolves the issue, and your best way forward in the moment may still be to find a new tribe or a new position. The real change has to come in longer-term strategies that change understanding, behavior, and outcomes. And the best way to change the outcomes is to create awareness around the issue and then seek solutions that create a win-win for all parties. But in culture, we call Matthew 18, mediation. The foundation of mediation is in essence the Matthew 18 process, though now it includes an agreement up front in work environments that you and the party you are not agreeing with will abide by the mediator's decision. In business, having hard conversations and helping others come to agreement is not considered an out of the ordinary process or event, at least not as much so as in many churches. Why? There are many possibilities but, in my experience, they were either grounded in fear or pride.

To walk in true freedom, restoration and often healing is also required. We know from Scripture that the truth sets you free (John 18:32). And knowing the truth definitely does that! But often you will never know the whole truth. People who behave badly, many times won't admit wrongdoing, and as I've mentioned, many of the guys refuse the Matthew 18 process. So how do you move on when you can't have a conversation about what really happened or come to any agreement? In my case, I had very healthy conversations with my own pastor, and I was grateful, despite disagreeing with some of his answers, that we could do that. But in many other cases, when I was not able to have those conversations, I had to let things go and try and move on without resolve. But that is much harder to do.

Faith requires you to trust God with the outcome and forgiveness is key to moving on.

In some of the experiences I had around the limiting belief system in churches, I found that many times when there were two or more parties at odds with each other, especially when the conflict was between a man and a woman, the men were given grace while the women were not. The answer I regularly received when I would question the way that things were handled was always, 100% of the time, *we need to just give people grace.* At first, I accepted the answer on face value, even at times feeling shame that I had a hard time giving grace when awful people committed harm and would refuse to try and work things out. But over time I learned to understand the grace they were dispensing was subjective and based on who you were, what circles you were in, and often, based on how righteousness you were deemed to be. So God took me on a deep dive around the concept of grace so that I could be better about giving it, but also be able to speak to it when it was used discriminately, or worst, when the gift of grace was converted back to a requirement to earn it.

Grace is the power of God working in you to help you have a transformed life and cannot be earned. The whole point is that it is a gift, not a result of privilege or position. In 2 Corinthians 12:7-10 how Paul describes it, "Therefore, in order to keep me from becoming conceited, I was given a thorn in my flesh, a messenger of Satan, to torment me. Three times I pleaded with the Lord to take it away from me. But he said to me, "My grace is sufficient for you, for my power is made perfect in weakness." Therefore I will boast all the more gladly about my weaknesses, so that Christ's power may rest on me. That is why, for Christ's sake, I delight in weaknesses, in insults, in hardships, in persecutions, in difficulties. For when I am weak, then I am strong."

We also see in Ephesians 2:8-9, that God gives grace through faith as a gift to believers. "For it is by grace you have been saved, through faith and this is not from yourselves; it is the gift of God - not by works, so that no one can boast". But in James 2:20-22, we see Paul explaining that faith without action is "useless", "You foolish person, do you want evidence that faith without deeds is useless? Was not our father Abraham considered righteous for what he did when he offered his son Isaac on the alter? You see that his faith and his actions were working together, and his faith was made complete for what he did."

God's grace is usually defined as underserved favor, forgiveness of our sins through the redemption of Jesus Christ. This principle is tough to accept, especially for women, when grace is dispensed disproportionately to men. But ultimately, only God can restore what has been lost and you and I cannot control the outcomes of situations where one of the parties does not want to work things out. In a perfect church, pastors, and leaders, would respond to every word that casts doubt about another person, even when wrapped in prayer, and every piece of gossip or warning about another believer, with "let's go talk with them together". But instead, the accusations, backstabbing, gossip, and splitting is very often accepted as truth. And in order for you to move on, you will likely have to let it go with no resolution and move on, giving the person grace and forgiving them, allowing God to provide the action. This is what I, and many other women I know, have to do. Today, many of the people I encountered that used limiting behaviors against me and other women, are still doing it, and many people I once called friends, are still believing lies about you and me. But God knows the truth and we have to let Him do what He does. "For if you forgive other people when they sin against you, your heavenly Father will also forgive you. But if you do not forgive others their sins, your Father will not forgive your sins" Matthew 6:14-15.

The last step of restoration was for me to really understand how to move forward with a clear understanding of what was happening to I could respond better in the future. In the first examples I gave of my bosses harming myself and others, their belief systems were grounded in their power and their inability to separate their egos from their titles. And they were behaving poorly. I can't really assess where they got their beliefs, but I do know that the belief system at the time in culture rewarded aggressive behavior from men in positions of authority towards women. So what about the limiting belief system in the church? The main behaviors that are used against women, say we should remain silent, ask our husbands when we have a question about Scripture, that we cannot lead in churches, and we cannot lead in culture. I and other women I know in leadership, in both the church and culture, definitely have many examples of men telling them to remain silent. In my work examples early in life, my boss specifically used this language regularly when we were in conversations.

You are hopefully now on your way to reconciling the truth and the lies, and you are beginning to get on good footing again, having started the process of healing. During the final parts of my refining season as the pandemic hit in 2020, God began to restore so many personal parts of my life that it's hard for me to explain it well to you, but I'm going to try. There came a point that I had exhausted every avenue I had to heal that I could do alone. Of course, my amazing husband and family, were with me and a great source of comfort. But I'm not the first leader to have been through a tough season. So God began to bring both new people into my life that could speak to what I had experienced, and he brought some old friends back into my life who unbeknownst to me were experiencing similar things at the same time I was. But the consistent and confirming message was the same, "it's not fair, it's not fun to go through, but you have to let it go and let God handle it from here". The second part of the message was, have you been through healing? And so, I began to seek out believers who were experienced and have the gift of healing to work through and find freedom from the things that were still keeping me bound.

I received great wisdom from counselors who told me to be more discerning about who I allowed into my circles and not to agree to sit at every table or be led by every leader. And I received prophetic words with some of that counsel, including from one prophet who told me to be careful which tables I sit at. He reminded me that round tables are meant for collaboration, but rectangle tables are meant for governing. He, of course, was referencing a spiritual meaning of the table. But the timing of the word and the point of it was to remind me that my input, voice, and position are valuable and should be honored and not just to collaborate but to govern. Most women don't realize they've been invited to a round table, not a rectangle table. This prophet reminded me that God would show me, if I asked Him, which tables to sit at and which ones to politely decline.

I also sought out healing from several sources, all who had trained in their gift, and were referred to me. I will caution you that for the same reasons you should not sit at every table, you should be careful who you choose to enter into healing with. Get some good names from trusted sources. During prayer and healing sessions, I was able to hear some things from God about past decisions and relationships that I had thought were long forgotten and He was able to bring deep healing by sharing these things through words of knowledge with people I didn't know. No one knew these things and they couldn't have known, not only about the experiences themselves, but how God worked with me personally for healing. They confirmed what I already knew from God. And lastly, God even showed me through others that had dealt with some of the same people I had, that some of them had done exactly the same types of things to them as they did to me, down to the detail. A few of the experiences I had were so personal and the people who perpetrated them are so known that I cannot share them for fear of retribution, including in this book, but God still restored my faith in Him by dealing with it personally.

Now that God had helped me to heal, I could begin to consider how to move forward and rebuild the things that He called me to. I was reminded that in Zechariah 9:12, God promised He would restore double what the enemy took, "Return to your fortress, you prisoners of hope; even now I announce that I will restore twice as much to you, it's taken me a while to believe this. But one of the first things He did is come to me in a dream and let me know that I was going to be moving into teaching others to do what I had done in ministry, and that I would do it through writing and speaking. He gave me more detail than that, but I'll reserve some of that between me and Him. In early 2021 I was offered an opportunity to start a position at a Christian University as an Adjunct Professor (part of the pool of part-time professors) and I began to get trained how to teach and how to regain my teaching voice. And after teaching multiple classes in the business school, He settled me into teaching Leadership and Ethics, and Entrepreneurship. And He continued to remind me that training others was something that I really loved to do. And now I understood that He had wired me to be an apostolic leader who could receive His blueprints, build according to plan, see the gold in people, help place them in position and help others be set free by breaking off many of the burdens they carry and contend for supernatural healing. I didn't realize at this point, the depth of training He still had for me in these things, but I'm sharing His promises to me so that hopefully you can see how He wants to do the same for you. He just wants you to trust Him to get you there, and I know He will.

Reconciling all of these things is a lot! It's hard to bring light to an issue that most of us don't want to talk about. But the truth is, in order to see change for us as women and for our sons and daughters, we have to address it, and we have to do it in a way that is consistent with His Word. The whole point of God sending Jesus was to reconcile all of us to God, giving us direct access to Him through our belief in Jesus. No one can take that away from you and me. As you do this, you will see the past reconciled, your healing recognized and the freedom to move into the future of your own calling. It will continue to be hard at times and require you to remain in Him, but it's worth it. Now it's time to look forward and discover and develop your mantles, including how God has wired you to use your voice, innovation, and creativity, as He refines and nurtures your leadership.

Reflection

1. What types of limits have you encountered in your own leadership settings?
2. Have you ever been refused a reconciliation meeting?
3. Have you ever considered what the message is that you are called to preach?
4. Have you ever been called by God to something only you could do and if so, how did you know it was from Him?
5. What is your calling?

CHAPTER 12

THE POWER OF HER MANTLES

"So Elijah went from there and found Elisha son of Shaphat. He was plowing with twelve yoke of oxen, and he himself was driving the twelfth pair. Elijah went up to him and threw his cloak around him. Elisha then left his oxen and ran after Elijah. "Let me kiss my father and mother goodbye," he said, "and then I will come with you."

—I KINGS 19:19-21

The power of your mantle or calling is that it comes from God, is walked out in partnership with Jesus and is empowered by the Holy Spirit. A mantle is defined by gotquestions.org as a covering such as a cloak, robe, or other article of clothing. The mantle is a symbolic and physical reminder of a calling from God and wrapped in His authority. For some the mantle is passed down and for others it is developed by God to be the breaker and pioneer of a new spiritual legacy. Mantle and anointing are words that often get used interchangeably, but there is a distinction between them. Anointing comes from the Holy Spirit and is the power that one needs to complete the calling. Mantles can take time to develop and often require identity development and mentoring, while anointing is a transfer from a higher authority and can happen suddenly. For instance, when Elijah passed his mantle onto Elisha in 1 Kings 19:19-21 this was a physical gesture of him passing down his prophetic office, but it was also symbolic of the Holy Spirit. Regardless of the way you receive the mantle or anointing, it comes from God, and you need the power of the Holy Spirit to fully walk in it.

There came a moment when I recognized that the ministry, I was leading was powerless and ineffective in restoring people in the way that I felt God wanted for them. I had developed programs and models and even physical homes for people who were being rescued from sex trafficking, homelessness, and poverty. But as soon as I and the team addressed one issue another one would arise. And while God does give us a roadmap for how to serve the poor for example, there was something missing. What I now understand is that first, I believed the only way I could receive a mantle was from my pastor. I had watched pastors pass down their titles and positions to other men, and rarely to women. And I knew that my own pastor would not lay hands on me and commission me into my calling into ministry, because of the limiting belief system of the church. And second, I was not yet operating fully in the gift of the Holy Spirit. I now understand that I was not only focused on the wrong things, but that I was still in a testing and refining season, and that though I had heard correctly regarding my calling, I was not fully operating in the anointing.

As I have discussed I did not really have the power of the Holy Spirit operating fully until 2020 just when the ministry was preparing to close down. But once I did get an opportunity to take that new gifting and test it in ministry, I realized that though we were feeding the hungry or the poor, we were not setting them free or removing the yoke of oppression from them. We were sharing religion but not sharing the power of the Holy Spirit. I had received the calling from God, but I did not have the anointing of the Holy Spirit to complete it. Isaiah 61:1 says, "The Spirit of the Sovereign Lord is on me, because the Lord has anointed me to proclaim good news to the poor. He has sent me to bind up the brokenhearted, to proclaim freedom for the captives and release from darkness for the prisoners." Yes, I was called to unite the Church in order to see those things become something churches did together. But ultimately, I knew prophetically that God did not call me or His Church to cause people's oppression to be worst when we engaged them. The point was to set people free. And I wanted to understand how to do that.

One of the ways God helps us begin to see what He is calling us to do, as I've mentioned, is through our journey, design, and spiritual gifts, and how they operate such as physical hearing, seeing, knowing, understanding, or feeling God. Others are through dreams, visions, pictures, or other encounters. We can see themes or threads that are repeated or highlighted to us. For instance, if you have one of the speaking gifts (teaching, exhortation, etc.), God may be calling you to preach or be a pastor. Or if you have the gift of teacher then you are likely called to teach but it can be anywhere such as in education, business, academia, or as a pastor. These are hints to where God wants to use us. 1 Peter 4:10 says, "As each one has received a special gift, employ it in serving one another, as good stewards of the manifold grace of God." A good steward is one who employs his gifts (accepts his mantle) by faithful development (training and use).

When the pandemic hit, I was forced to really reconcile the things that happened in ministry, connect the dots to some of the hang ups that I had carried for much of my life, and allow God to begin to restore me to His design for me. "But I will restore you to health and heal your wounds,' declares the LORD, 'because you are called an outcast, Zion, for whom no one cares." Jeremiah 30:17. And though I had done the work to bring healing, restoration requires rest. I was wounded and had a lot of traumas from some of the experiences, especially from 2017-2020. But I also had to reconcile what God called me to. After questioning everything, I realized that I didn't know how to trust God again, when He seemingly called me and failed to protect me. And part of me having my mantles refined and restored was for Him to rebuild my faith.

I believe that the reason the Holy Spirit moved us out of our church and into a new one, was so I could be discipled by Him to receive the fullness of my calling and mantle, so that He could establish in me something I couldn't see or receive in the place we were. And, because of the way I'm wired, apostolically and entrepreneurially, of course He was going to ask me to start something new! I know that may seem obvious to you as you have read about my journey, but it wasn't to me then. And because our mantles are established first personally through our own identity and purpose, they also have to be established corporately through our leadership and calling. Our goal as believers, is to pursue and identify what our mantles are, steward them well and then hopefully, pass them on to our family and others respectively. But, understanding what God is asking you to do and knowing what steps to take to get there, are two very different levels of faith, though God will build both.

One night in July 2021, I went to sleep like any other night except that we had just found out that our oldest daughter was pregnant. We were so excited to meet our first grandchild! We were on the other side of most of the journey I have described, and God was rebuilding our trust in His promises, but we were still in the middle of a pandemic. What I didn't know yet was that our daughter would get COVID at eleven weeks of pregnancy and that my husband would almost die from it. It was too early to know what sex the baby was, and I was historically terrible at guessing that outcome. But that night, God wanted to instill in me and us as a family that the things we had gone through had purpose and that He was going to restore all that was lost, including the legacy of our family and our daughters. For the rest of the night, for eight full hours, I dreamt about our soon-to-be granddaughter. She was beautiful and had wispy hair like her father and blue eyes. She gazed into my eyes all night as she grew from birth and into a young woman. She was so smart, and we talked about everything. I woke up the next morning knowing that I had had a prophetic dream, the longest one by far that I had ever had. This wasn't like the dreams I had when I asked God to take them away where I was dreaming of future events and hovering over them trying to save them. But it was the first dream of its length since that time only this time it was giving me a future glimpse of life! I knew by now that prophetic dreams were different in that they were forever etched in me, and they had the fingerprints of God on them that left resin from His presence. I knew that morning that God would protect our family unit and that despite what would come just a couple of months later, with the onset of covid, our family would be blessed and protected and that the dream would serve as a reminder as we walked through some challenges leading up to her birth. I also believed at the time that the dream was not just to help rebuild my faith but that of my family, so I told all of them about the dream, trusting God with the outcome. A month later, the ultrasound confirmed it was a girl, and then as she was born and continues to grow, I marvel at how much she looks and has the personality exactly as I dreamed. Since then, and at the final edit of this writing, I have now had a second dream about our second grandchild and it has now been confirmed, it is a boy, just like in my second dream. God is serious about restoring our family. And He's just as serious about yours!

I was beginning to believe more and more that God, in His great mercy and understanding, was going to restore all things to us that were seemingly lost during the refining season, including our family legacy. Legacy, the mantle you get to pass on, is defined in the secular world by a person leaving property, money, or even pain and suffering to the next generation. In the Bible, legacy is more focused on how we build into the next generation from a perspective of passing on our inheritance in the Lord in terms of salvation and biblical teaching. Biblical legacy is also focused on spiritual things like passing on the fruit of the Spirit, which means the Holy Spirit's gifts and graces, including how to use them, but it can also include the consequences of sin. For those of you who have traumas that you experienced in the past you understand that it effects how you operate, how you perceive life, whether you succeed or not? Women seem to understand this sometimes more than men. We know that when the hearts of our daughters and sons, sisters, and mothers and fathers are hurt, or when women are physically harmed, it affects the outcomes of their lives for seasons and generations to come. And we know instinctively that if those traumas are not healed, they not only get passed on to the next generation, but the victim of the abuse may never live the life they were intended and designed to live. So legacy matters!

The good news is, we can break off these old patterns of behavior and usher in new ones of blessing. The reason that those consequences of sin keep returning is because they are familiar to us, and we accept them back in. Familiar spirits are another demonic spirit that will use the familiar things in our family to get us to agree with false beliefs that we have grown comfortable with. Examples of this are alcoholism or addiction, and the behavior could be co-dependency that keeps you bound. Another example is when we consult mediums or fortune tellers or tarot cards, in order to talk to our deceased family members. In Deuteronomy 18:10-11, we see God warning us, "Let no one be found among you who sacrifices their son or daughter in the fire, who practices divination or sorcery, interprets omens, engages in witchcraft, or casts spells, or who is a medium or spiritist or who consults the dead." These are all ways the enemy again uses the things that you are vulnerable in to get you to partner with those behaviors again. Blessing, on the other hand, is passing on God's intended outcomes, which include identity, healing, and freedom in Christ.

Some of my familial history wasn't always optimal, and for many of us there will be things we want to carry into the next generations and other things we won't.

We can also choose to partner with the Holy Spirit and break off the things that need to go and train and empower our children with the things we want to be carried on into the next generations. God knew that it mattered to both my husband and me that we wanted to leave some things behind and at the same time shift our family's future. The single most important factor in your life that insures you get to continue in your own spiritual familial legacy is your own parents. And for many people, that may not be a source of comfort for you. The good news is that regardless of your past, God can restore you and your future family legacy, while reconciling the past one. This is one of the reasons that Jesus and how He is reflected in churches is so important and has huge ramifications if not done in a healthy way. One of the most important relationships you can have is with other believers who can help you personally and corporately both develop and establish you from identity to calling. But when that goes wrong, you're not just contending for your own healing, you often will have to contend for that of your family.

Our children are adults now, but in 2009 when I started the ministry and the first challenge came when we lost most of our financial resources through fraud by someone they knew in the church, it put in motion their own version of the truth. And because my husband and I didn't even recognize what was happening to us, we weren't equipped to help them either, except to be honest and share with them truthfully what was happening, including our anger and our tears, and the moments of clarity and healing. It is why God knew the dream of our granddaughter was so much more than just a dream to us! Legacy helps build success into the next generation and equips others to better handle the things that life brings better than if they knew nothing. Psalm 78:4 says, "We will not hide them from their descendants; we will tell the next generation the praiseworthy deeds of the Lord, his power, and the wonders he has done." Our family legacy is an important mantle we are all called to.

One of the ways that you can leave an inheritance to those in your own family, as well as, others you meet along the way, is through mentoring, discipleship, and spiritual mothering. In future chapters, I will touch more on mentoring, but the term spiritual mothering, a form of personal discipleship, is another principle that I had never considered or heard of prior to the refinement portion of my ministry journey. I was blessed to have been a part of a group of mature women who understood who they were to God, and how to see others through His eyes. Those women, who I will share more about in future chapters, demonstrated to me how to hear God for others and how to help others see God in them. A spiritual mother is intentionally helping others see the same in themselves. This book, in my own way, will hopefully help you see yourself differently than you did before, in a way that honors God's promises to you as His daughter. But spiritual mothering is more than that. It is personal discipleship and pouring into others specifically with the feminine heart of God. Part of our legacy is to leave what we have learned to our biological family, but it is also to leave the same to others we meet along the way. Your most important mantle is your family!

The second area that God restored my understanding in, specifically when it comes to mantles, is that often mantles are given to you and then as part of the refining process, they are taken away. Joseph was given a coat of many colors, and His destiny was prophesied to him, but then his brothers became jealous of that mantle and took it from him literally. Joseph had to go through a refinement season and some trials of his own before that mantle was anointed by God and brought into its fullness. In my season, as you may have also experienced, you might have thought that your mantle was stolen, lost, or robbed, as I did. And you may be questioning God as to why He would put you into position only to have it taken from you so harshly. But only God sees the big picture, from Heaven's perspective.

And when it's time He will reveal to you what He is up to, and He will redeem those trials, even the failures, and restore them for you.

As you receive the mantles that God has for you, He will show you spiritually why He is giving them to you, and you will likely also hear confirmation from others. Ask the Holy Spirit to help you determine what that looks like for you. And don't get too caught up in the title or the type of mantle, each one is given as a gift, meaning God wants to give you exactly what you have hoped it would be! Except He will give to you in the most personal and beautiful way that only He and you know just how perfect for you it is. When you receive it, you will know it is for you and that it is from Him. And you will want to both steward it and pass it on to others, as a part of your intentional leadership role, whether it's in your family, your church or in culture. Next, He began to develop and establish my leadership through innovation and creativity, as He will do for you too.

Reflection

1. What themes do you see in your family legacy, both positive and negative?
2. What tools from the Bible do you now have that can help you shift your family in a positive direction?
3. What things have you accepted, if any, that you see having a more negative outcome on your family than positive?
4. What positive outcomes do you see in your family line? Are you intentional about making sure those things get passed on to your children?
5. Have you ever had a female spiritual mentor? How would it feel different than having a male one?

CHAPTER 13

THE POWER OF HER INNOVATION

"And no one pours new wine into old wineskins. Otherwise, the wine will burst the skins, and both the wine and the wineskins will be ruined. No, they pour new wine into new wineskins."

—MARK 2:22

The power of innovation is having the freedom to create what only you are designed and purposed to do. Innovation is defined by Merriam Webster[13] as, a new idea, method, or device; or the introduction of something new. That freedom allows you to dream big dreams and create, innovate, and bring solutions that solve problems for the world. God was the first founder and CEO, and as He created His vision for the world, He placed free will and purpose in each of us.

What dream has God placed in you? Though we all have innovation and creativity in us, some of us are carrying someone else's vision, while others don't even believe that God wants us to be part of His plan at all! The truth is that our identity, purpose, leadership, and kingdom calling are what draw us to God in a tangible way, making His Word come alive during our journey in life.

When you are doing what you are purposed to do,
you will wake up every morning with endless energy.
But when you are carrying someone else's
why, you will burn out quickly.

Well into the final season of my journey in 2020, other women leaders and I were beginning to meet and discuss under our breath our continued desire to bring together diverse Christian leaders from churches, nonprofits, and marketplace businesses around solutions to social issues and causes in the region. We were frustrated that following the various meetings we often attended with men, that we found ourselves not being included as the plans moved forward. As a result, we concluded that if we set up meetings with the right people, meaning people who were more used to seeing women lead, and were intentional about ensuring that they were diverse, the outcome would be different. So we gathered together with eight men and women, diverse in age and ethnicity, whom we had identified as business leaders and mature believers. We started the discussion with each person at the table providing their input on what we believed the Church together could accomplish in our region specifically around innovation, how we could all help in our respective areas, and what strategies we could use to implement those strategies collectively. The women at the table came prepared with well thought out recommendations, something that is not uncommon in leadership circles. The men were not as prepared but quickly presented their ideas. As the meeting progressed, right before our eyes, the women's well-prepared recommendations became the men's ideas. And then, as we discussed the next steps, one of the men looked at the other men at the table and announced the next step should be that those three men in the group should meet to discuss how to implement the ideas the women had brought to the table. In an award-winning moment, one of the women, a beautiful, powerful woman of God, stood up and said to the men, "Did you really just do that?!?" The men were oblivious. They had blank stares and even after explaining how they'd overtaken the meeting; they could not see it. We never met again in that group.

The truth is that what we experienced that day was not an uncommon scenario; we had attended many other meetings like it before. Men leaders often don't recognize what they are doing, and even when it is pointed out to them, they can't see it and emphatically argue it meant nothing and they didn't do anything wrong. The challenge then is, how do we move into leadership and calling when we cannot partner with the men involved? Most women I meet are tired of talking about it and tired of waiting for the guys to change. If you're like me, I don't walk into these types of meetings today having a lot of hope things will be different. At the same time, I'm married to a man who does not engage women this way at all, so I know they are out there! Let's see if the next phase of the framework brings any more clarification and can help to guide us to a solution.

One of the businesses that I developed out of a need we saw for the ministry, was to help incubate leaders and kingdom minded businesses. God gave me a dream for a commercial real estate building where we could share space and develop best practices together. I, and my team, developed an ecosystem of believers who were working together, worshiping together, equipping each other, and helping one another build and execute their respective visions. Within that space I also developed social purpose incubator and accelerator programs that would help entrepreneurs validate their ideas, launch their businesses, and/or scale their companies while at the same time having an impact on their community through their efforts. After working with hundreds of soon-to-be or existing founders, something started to happen that I didn't expect. Almost 50 percent of the business owners either changed their ideas or closed their businesses, following the program. Why? Because they were carrying someone else's vision or because they had never considered that there was a vision in them at all.

During this same season, I came to work with endless energy every day excited to see what God was going to do next. One of my favorite things to do is to help others see God's vision for them and their calling. But as we saw in the framework, God also does everything in season and in His timing. I was so caught up in the excitement of the moment, I made decisions I would have never made in the business world, including who my partners would be and if they had also been truly called to my vision. So when money became tight and we hit the first hint of spiritual warfare, each one of them reacted out of their own fear and did things that were not in character with who God designed them to be. The vision God trusted me with was never theirs to carry, and I learned an important lesson about how to protect what God has given you. I also learned the importance of making sure that before you try to partner with others, you and they need to know who they are and what God has called them to. It's one of the reasons why I'm so passionate about identity and kingdom calling today.

At the same time, innovation is dependent on an ecosystem of like-minded people who honor and trust each other with their visions and dreams. Freedom is also required for creativity, innovation, and entrepreneurship. In innovation circles in the business world today, there is an understanding based on experience that the more diverse your team of innovators and creators are, the better the ideas and outcomes are, both socially and financially. Much of the ongoing success of Silicon Valley is their ability to bring in the nobodies and turn them into somebodies. The person with no title is just as important to the process as the ones with the titles. It looks similar to the way God designed us all to operate in His kingdom. In 1 Corinthians

13:9-12 it says, "For we know in part, and we prophesy in part, but when completeness comes, what is in part disappears. When I was a child, I talked like a child, I thought like a child, I reasoned like a child. When I became a man, I put the ways of childhood behind me. For now we see only a reflection as in a mirror; then we shall see face to face. Now I know in part; then I shall know fully, even as I am fully known." In the same way that we are all necessary parts of God's body of believers, relative to identity and purpose, our ideas are meant to be part of God's full solution. But we need each other.

The purpose of innovation is to bring a solution to a problem. What problem are you trying to solve? What solution do you have for that problem? In the kingdom, the focus is on the solution and the result is both financial and spiritual. And it requires, the Holy Spirit to guide you on what seasons, purposes and outcomes, God has for the time. Remember this is a kingdom blueprint for something God is calling you to. He's going to give you a solution that is unique to His nature. What is unique about this solution? You are what makes this idea different from someone else's, so what do you bring to the table that no one else can? Who is this solution designed for? Who are your customers or the people you will serve? How does God want you to pay for it? What expenses will you have? And finally, what are the outcomes you expect to have and what biblical principles will you use to build the blueprint, initiative, or organization? So for example, maybe God gave you a vision for a faith-based mediation program to use in churches, and you want to use Matthew 18 as the model for it. If you were to read all of Matthew 18, you would discover God's blueprint for how to engage fairly with each other, and you might decide to launch a version of it. Some of the greatest untapped potential in the Church today, besides women, are businesspeople and specifically entrepreneurs who also struggle with what their place is in the Church. God wants His entire Church engaged and operating in His design for them. What would it look like to have everyone in the Church understanding who they are and each doing their part?

Because Church unity is a passion of mine, I want to spend just a few minutes on it, though God was clear with me that this book was for women and that women had to take their place first, before the Church would be effective at unity. Many in the Church today, like I was and maybe like you, are not established in their personal and spiritual identity, purpose, and calling; this inhibits unity in the Church. But I have still seen glimpses of unity, and there is a common thread when I have: the people involved have gone through the refining fire and are mature in their identity, purpose, and calling. Unity in the Church, then, becomes an outcome of all believers operating in their identity, purpose, and calling. And the Holy Spirit releases unity and blessing, which demonstrates to the world that God is real and that He loves us and Him. This is our testimony! The world needs to see that we can be unified in the Spirit. Unity is not all of us doing, being, and thinking the same thing. Unity is exactly the opposite of that. Unity embraces the unique and divine callings, characters, and assignments of all members in the body of Christ working together, as one unit in the Spirit, toward one goal, sharing Christ's love and showing the world He is alive. God has the master plan! And when each of us discovers what our true calling is, it will be nothing like that of our neighbor! When you step into that, your relationship with God takes on a whole new meaning. It becomes real, maybe for the first time, that God actually does know every hair on your head and cares about you individually in ways that only He could. But we have to find who we are first and walk in that identity so that He can guide us into our purpose. And again, it's completely contrary to Scripture to say He will only do this with men. He loves all of us and has put purpose in each of us. In Scripture, God often used women to birth change, sometimes literally, as in Mary's case. Innovation and entrepreneurship are great ways for change to happen.

I have seen and experienced so many unique ideas in our incubator and ministry season, often from people and organizations you will likely never hear about. But I want to plant seeds of hope about your unique purpose and calling by highlighting some of them. I have definitely seen solutions to homelessness that work and that wholistically not only provide housing but restore and heal people. I've seen answers to sexual exploitation and have seem women who are restored become successful advocates for ending sex trafficking and other forms of abuse. I've seen groups of intercessors whose purpose is to intercede for and ask the Holy Spirit with success where to find missing children. And then have successful relationships with law enforcement to find those children. And I've seen physical addiction and physical ailments healed right before my eyes. Whatever God has placed in you, He can do it, through you.

I hope you are beginning to dream about what you and God are going to build together! It's so much fun watching people like you learn to hear from God and understand Him better, and then getting more and more downloads from Him of vision and revelation of things that you may have never seen before. But I have also learned through experience that most people will not execute a vision without help from a mentor. Because women, much more than men, do not have access to or often get to work with mentors, I wanted to infuse some wisdom on this topic to help you get started. First, mentors are not coaches. Coaches empower you, but mentors equip you and teach you from experience. If your mentor has not done what you want to do multiple times, they are probably not going to be helpful enough to get you launched, and you will spend a lot of time figuring things out. A mentor should minimize the things you have to figure out and make your time more efficient. Second, if you get an opportunity to have a male mentor, you should not necessarily turn it down, but just recognize they are going to mentor you from a male lens. I highly recommend also seeking out a female mentor, who will be able to mentor you from a female lens. Women who have been there don't just mentor you on your way toward starting and building your blueprint but also on what you will experience, especially as women, as you move into ownership, leadership, and position.

In addition to mentorship, there are other helpful avenues to better prepare you to launch your ideas and dreams. Incubator programs operate like mentors but in a programmed group environment specifically designed to help you launch or grow your business. Incubators often provide education, access to other founders, opportunities to share your ideas with others, funding, speaking, and access to other men and women with the experience. Dreaming is fun, and coming up with a vision is not that difficult when you are given the right questions and allowed to answer from personal experiences. But mentors will help you fill in the blanks by providing the steps you can take based on their experience and knowledge, and that's the hard part. In a similar way, only you can add the detail to your P.I.N.K. framework, but a mentor can help extract that from inside of you and give you the steps to take to move forward more efficiently. The framework helps you focus on the right things, while your relationship with Jesus and the guidance of the Holy Spirit will help you understand. And God always brings other people to complete what He has first shared with you. Mentoring can help us do that by pointing us in the right direction and giving us strategies to the challenges we will face that are unique to women.

Finally, I want to leave you with this caution. I did not realize until recently that part of the underlying limiting belief system that I believed for so long, had created in me a co-dependency requiring a man to give me approval of or join my effort, before I could move forward. I'm not suggesting you can't have great male partners and support. But I am cautioning you, if you were raised in the limiting belief system like I was, you may still be under the assumption that men owe it to you to help you start what God is calling you alone to start. Again, it doesn't mean you can't have men investing in you; it's the heart around the support that matters. God will equip you, fund you, and stand with you as you move forward, and for some of you, God may not let you partner with men again until you partner with Him first and He shows you how to take the lead. This is what He did for me.

The power of being free enough to innovate is you get to not only choose what to participate in, but whether to participate or not. You get to choose your future, and you don't need permission to be who God has called you to be in the church or otherwise. You get to help create change for others. What has God placed in you that no one else can do? You are uniquely qualified to see your vision recognized, and only you get to decide if it moves forward. And though others may seem like their vision is the same as your vision, please do not let that stop you. I have often seen God bring two or more people together who thought they were moving in the same direction, doing the same work, finally partner together, only to discover that God was partnering them so that they each could get something God wanted them to have from the other. And if they had stopped short in fear of not having heard from God what they thought they heard, or it not being as unique as they thought it should be, they would have missed out on walking out their mission hand in hand with Jesus by their side, as he not only develops and establishes your creativity and innovation but your voice. Your personal voice becomes refined into your purposeful voice when God takes what's in you and partners it with action.

Reflection

1. What would you create if money, resources, and time was not a hindrance?
2. What is an example of an ecosystem?
3. What dreams have you set aside thinking God would never use you that way?
4. Have you ever considered what steps you would take to start a company with your own ideas?
5. What would that look like? If you're not sure, ask the Holy Spirit to help you.

CHAPTER 14

THE POWER OF HER PROPHETIC VOICE

*"Follow the way of love and eagerly desire
gifts of the Spirit, especially prophecy."*

—1 CORINTHIANS 14:1

The power of your prophetic voice is being able to speak life into others by hearing from God and having others do the same for you with freedom and in the fullness of who He is. It is also the unique message that represents Jesus in you. Your voice is part of the way that God develops leadership in you. As you speak to others and they respond, or not, it sharpens your message. The enemy's plan all along was to take my voice. It's one of the most powerful tools God gives us to reach others. It's no wonder, then, that the strategy he would use would be to ensure that I could not speak. And because we know that the enemy always uses strategies that twists what God says or does, the shutting down of my voice was done in a way that was wrapped with twisted scriptures about women being silent. There came a point when I had believed so many lies, and the enemy was attacking so hard, I could say virtually nothing in conversations and people walked away offended. I had spent most of my life having a huge circle of friends and was known as the person who could invite hundreds of people to my home, and they would all show up tomorrow. But by the time I transitioned my businesses, and God called us out of our church of over fifteen years, that circle had grown very small, and my confidence was at an all-time low. I felt rejected, accused, and betrayed, and I trusted almost no one. But God had been training me to understand my spiritual identity and understand the spiritual gifts, including the gift of prophecy. And the prophetic words that I received during this season were a lifeline. They hit the target so well that I knew it was from God. And that is what kept me going. I had a dear friend of mine with an office in our hub who would call me or check on me almost daily and pour God's promises into me, and she always had a prophetic word for me, including one for this book and how I would write it in a specific way that has now come to fruition.

One day another friend called me and asked if I would be willing to meet once a month with a group of diverse women soon form-ing to "minister" to each other. I didn't really understand what that meant at the time, except I assumed it included prophecy, so I agreed to show up and check it out. God knew I needed to hear more women's voices who were experiencing more of Him, and this group was exactly that. We first met in 2019 but I continue to meet together with many of them today. For one of the first times in my life, maybe the only time in a circle of women, we didn't talk about where we worked or our titles; we just started praying together and "ministering" to each other in the Spirit. We only met once a month, but it was like we had always known each other. We almost instantly knew each other through our spiritual identities, the way God sees and knows us. And as we met, we got to know each other's unique voices and unique combinations of spiritual gifts that made us very distinct from each other.

Your voice is a product of Jesus in you and flows out of your personal identity, purpose, leadership, and calling, along with how you uniquely operate in your fivefold grace and spiritual gifts. In my experience with this group of women, some of us were and are seers, some hearers, some knowers, and some feelers in the way we hear from God. Most of us speak in tongues and operate strongly in prophecy. And some of our unique voices come through authoritative commands and declarations, singing, laughter, tears, discerning of spirits, healing, and deliverance. But what united us together was that we all understood and operated in our spiritual gifts at some level. I was so new to all of this, but God quickly anointed me in ways that helped me feel like I fit in. The longer the group met, the more I practiced my gifts and the more I began to develop my authentic voice.

As you may recall, prophecy is the ability to see, hear, feel, and know from God what He wants to communicate to others, and its purpose is to build up and equip the body of Christ. As God continued to refine me, the gift of prophecy moved from a list of gifts to a lifestyle of asking the Holy Spirit what to do or how to build others up in their faith. Jesus used prophecy to break through the systems of man by speaking what Father God would speak in a way they could not resist. Prophecy speaks life into people, and God will use you to speak into the lives of others. You may have been doing this for years and not understood what it was, like I did. I have always known things about other people, their thoughts and sometimes their inner struggles. I thought having this type of insight was something we could all do, though I now understand it is a gift that needs practice to steward well.

When you give a prophetic word, you are relying on the Holy Spirit to bring you the word. Because people sometimes give a word that is not from the Holy Spirit, it is dependent on you to discern if it confirms something you are already hearing from God or if not, you should let it go. But when God gives someone an authentic word for you, in my experience, He does it in a way that hits a target in you that only you know is there! And you will know if it's Him. The more I pressed into the gift, the louder and more accurate my voice became, while at the same time being grounded in the heart of the Father and love. Prophecy can include directional words for the future, a declaration, exhortation, instruction, or a prediction and is considered one of the speaking gifts from the list of spiritual gifts we've already learned about, but prophecy is specific to your voice, as are apostleship, teaching, evangelism, exhortation, discerning spirits, speaking in tongues, and interpreting tongues. In addition, the healing and deliverance ministry uses the gift of prophecy and discerning of spirits to heal or deliver us.

Because our voices represent Jesus in us, if your concept of Jesus is out of alignment with His Word, your voice will also be out of alignment. Our feminine voices not only sound different than the men's voices, in different octaves and patterns, but our language is also different. Our words and understanding of those words are different, and our messages are different. The lens that we look through is different, and that makes us see and think differently than men. The way that we present, argue, and get to the point are different. When women are together, we understand each other in a similar way that men do when they are together. It's painful to look back now and realize that most of my time in business and ministry, I was leading like a man instead of leading in a place that was authentically me. As a result, my leadership was firm and direct and sometimes more confrontational than it needed to be so that I could live up to all the training I had received that taught me to lead in a male-centric way. In the same way that I needed God to restore my feminine identity and purpose, I desperately needed to have my voice represent the authentic me. I could not "play the game" anymore. I couldn't pretend to be who I wasn't in settings that did not favor women. I needed to be able to stand up and declare, "You didn't just do that, did you?" like my friend did.

After spending eighteen months with this group of women that gathered to minister to each other, God had established and helped me see better who I was and developed my voice. Two years later, I'm still developing my voice further in partnership with the Holy Spirit and practicing my gifting. That process never ends. But the first step is to discover and establish your identity and purpose, and then start to practice your voice with a different mindset. I now understand that I experienced with these women, was a version of what is called a prophetic company. The first mention of a company of prophets is in 1 Samuel and was led by Samuel to deepen and extend the religious life among people. The point of the company of prophets was to train other prophets and have successors in prophetic office. They came together in unity to prophesy together in the times they were in and were strengthened by each other. Remember, we can all hear from God and operate in the gift of prophecy.

In 1 Samuel 10:5 it says, "Then Saul sent messengers to take David; and they saw a company of prophets prophesying, and Samuel standing as president over them; and the Spirit of God came upon the messengers of Saul, and they also prophesied. In 1 Kings, we see one of the company of prophets condemns Ahab. In 2 Kings the company of prophets came out and asked Elisha if he knew that the Lord was going to take his master from him that day. This is what we were doing in that group of women. We were building each other up with God's promises and His Word, sometimes offering healing and deliverance. Each woman was very distinct in her gifts and her voice. We met monthly and poured into each other by praying, prophesying over, and facilitating healing over each other. We also connected during the month over both good and bad things happening in our lives and prayed for each other in a symphony of prayer, while also sharing in each other's lives in a way that allowed us to call out and break off the presence of the enemy and his strategies.

The power of the group was in all of us operating in our spiritual gifts to build each other up and seeing the diversity I had read about in the Bible become real. We were so different in the Spirit there was no way or need to compare ourselves to each other. As a bonus, we didn't know each other prior to the group, so there were no preconceived opinions or experiences that hindered authenticity. Though eventually the group meetings came to a natural end, the relationships continue to this day. In addition to the group representing a diverse group of ages and ethnicity, the group also represented every aspect of the five-fold ministry, including a diverse set of ways that God spoke to each woman, as I've mentioned. Some of the women ministered through intercession, others through healing, others through leadership, and others through singing! We naturally fell into these roles in the group, and each of us was able to identify and help each other identify our graces and mantles. And we prophesied into them for each other for the future. The words that were spoken over me hit me in the Spirit, so I knew they were from God. They were not coming from a worldly perspective. Instead, they came from a spiritual perspective. So, as I worked out my spiritual identity by being in this group with mature women who understood their own identities, this is also the time that God put the Word in me. All these things together changed me and gave me the freedom that I live in today. I now understand that when the Bible says that the fruit of the Spirit is "of the Spirit," it means you won't experience it without the Spirit! And when Jesus prays for us to be "one in Spirit," we can't experience unity without the Holy Spirit! But I also understand that when I speak and people respond negatively for no apparent reason, it is sometimes me needing to have more grace, but it is a lot of times the enemy operating in others and responding to the gifts in me to see and have the authority to cause them to go. Finally, I needed all these things to find my voice and my message and be able to step into leadership again.

Now that I felt more equipped in hearing from God, He began to work on my message. The biggest change God brought to my perspective is to not limit myself to seeing only what is happening in my own life, or that of others, through a worldly perspective. But instead, He wanted me to understand His eternal design for women, and men, and to begin to live and see life through His lens with His mindset, a Kingdom one. Matthew 6:33 says, "But seek first his kingdom and his righteousness, and all these things will be given to you as well." In John 3:3, we read, "Jesus replied, "Very truly I tell you, no one can see the kingdom of God unless they are born again." And John 3:5-6, "Jesus answered, "Very truly I tell you, no one can enter the kingdom of God unless they are born of water and the Spirit. Flesh gives birth to flesh, but the Spirit gives birth to spirit." Romans 14:17, "For the kingdom of God is not a matter of eating and drinking, but of righteousness, peace and joy in the Holy Spirit." The Kingdom of God is all of God's creation, seeking Him in both the truth (Scripture) and in spirit (Holy Spirit), desiring to do His will, on earth as it is in heaven. Scripture is clear that pursuing what God desires is what He wants us to do! When your voice reflects the things that He desires coupled with what He has placed in you to be and do, your voice becomes a weapon against the enemy, to do God's will. We all have a voice and are called by God to use it for His purposes!

There was one more place of healing that I needed so that my voice could be released. And that was the fear that I had of speaking God's Word and being wrong. I had been so conditioned for so long that I wasn't chosen to preach or be a leader in the Church, I was afraid to step into it. But God had a plan for that too. He brings all things that He asks us to do full circle. In 2020, in the middle of the pandemic, when I was at one of my lowest points, a pastor friend of mine called me and asked if I would record a sermon for his church. I said, "You know I'm not a pastor and I've never preached a sermon, right?" He said, "I don't know what you are talking about, you've always been a pastor, and if you're up for it, I'd like to help videotape and produce your first sermon." He and his wife came over the next day, and in our living room, for an audience of four, I preached my first sermon on a topic I'm very fond of: identity. God is so good to us! It turns out that I've always had a message. But by now, I also had a deeper relationship with the Holy Spirit and the gift of prophecy, so my message had more power than the words alone in the way I would have spoken to them before. God used this moment to continue to restore my faith, reconcile my own journey, and restore my voice while refining my message.

We are all pastors and preachers in the context of the great commission. But we each have a different way of expressing our message. For some, it is in the church, others in business, or academia, or government, or the media for example. And some of our messages are delivered through speaking, teaching, singing, worshipping, training others, praying, etc. But we all have a voice, and we all have a message. But we also all have a testimony. And the testimony is what brings the power of the Holy Spirit and the deep relationship that was developed in you with God during your refining and testing season, to your ultimate message, as your journey becomes your testimony. Luke 8:39 says, "Return home and tell how much God has done for you." So the man went away and told all over town how much Jesus had done for him." Your testimony becomes the way that God takes what the enemy meant to destroy you and use it for good.

Reflection

1. Have you ever felt like you couldn't speak up? What have you done to overcome it?
2. What parts of your voice do you exercise most? Teaching? Singing? Writing? Preaching? Speaking? How does God ask you to verbalize his words to you?
3. What is your message?

4. Have you ever researched the spiritual history of your family? What did you find?
5. Have you ever considered your family's future spiritual legacy? What do you hope for?

CHAPTER 15

THE POWER OF HER NURTURED LEADERSHIP

"Do nothing out of selfish ambition or vain conceit. Rather, in humility value others above yourselves, not looking to your own interests but each of you to the interests of the others."

—PHILIPPIANS 2:3-4

The real power of leadership is recognized when you are able to operate fully and authentically in your own prophetic identity and incubated purpose, while at the same time you are able to empower others to discover and become established in theirs. When leaders walk into a position of power not having reached a place where they are mature in who they are, the pressure of leadership will cause the things that have still not been worked out to become multiplied when things get tough. Because women often don't have mentors to prepare us for those positions, when we step into leadership and face the first male leader who wants our position or who sees our natural disposition to build teams or have compassion for example, as a weakness, we are not equipped to handle the situation well. Jesus understood how to develop leaders by walking with them while also training them to do the same for others. Additionally, He knew that His authority came from God, not from the law, meaning that when God places you in position, His power and authority will follow. As we move into the next phase of the P.I.N.K. framework, we are going to shift our focus from our own personal identity, purpose, and leadership, now grounded in God's promises and design, to kingdom calling focused more corporately on serving others and His outcomes. As a believer, you're leadership positions, become your training ground that God uses not only to help refine you but to equip you to help refine others, as you move into your calling.

The process of refinement can be tough. I've often heard that if your refinement is longer or more intense, it's because you have so much to change, and maybe there is some truth to that. But in my experience and watching other people go through theirs, the journey corresponds to the calling. In other words, the journey, and the equipping for what you will need in your calling determine the length of the refinement and training. And we all go through a refinement process towards our calling, assuming you're pursuing it, regardless of where God has called you to serve. I thought that if I wanted to move into ministry that I had to do it in a church. But that is not consistent with God's Word! We are the church, in whatever sphere or position we hold. Where does God have you planted? In business? In the church? In the family? These are all important areas of calling that the Church often doesn't help us see is just as important to God as volunteering for ministry in the church.

The truth is most of us don't lead in the church. Instead, we lead where we work in areas of culture that have been identified generally as business, education, media, government, family, and entertainment. Each of these areas of culture have their own operating system and language. And God uses the fivefold leadership functions as the way you operate in the world, regardless of the area of culture. I also like to include nonprofits and health care as separate categories since they have their own languages and operating systems that differ from other areas of leadership. In business the language and motivation is often driven through action. Businesses exist to solve problems and make money. In education the motivation is teaching others. Media is about persuading others. Government is about managing society. Family is meant to empower each member, so the family functions well as a unit. Entertainment involves creating content that provides enjoyment for others. And we all lead in these areas every day, out of our natural strengths and personalities. But as believers we also lead out of the spiritual gifting that God placed in us at birth, whether we are aware of it or not. The more you understand your own gifting, the more you can authentically connect it to your leadership and calling. And those gifts are in operation whether you're in a church building or elsewhere. Apostolic people who are hardwired to create vision and build are often found in the business world where their gifting is more in alignment with the operating system of that area of culture. Teachers are often teachers in education. Evangelists are in almost every area of culture as the salespeople. Apostolic leaders, create vision and build things that have an eternal impact, such as healing identity, pointing people to calling, and setting the oppressed free. In business we call those things discovering your strengths, finding your purpose, and helping you heal from trauma. These are all things that we are asked to do as believers of Jesus. Because much of this is only discussed as happening inside a church building, however, we often don't feel like we're really called by God unless it's inside the church. But that was not God's intent. God helps us choose not only our careers and calling but He ordains our assignments and mantles specifically for us.

I no longer take every assignment that the world has to offer. I only take the ones that God says yes to. And when I take them, He honors this choice by both protecting me and empowering me in the assignment. He gives me favor to complete it and have the right connections while alerting me to the enemy's schemes so that I don't go through some of the things I have in the past. For example, I often get called to break ground spiritually so that change can occur, meaning that I will bring a caution to a church or organization or leader, that they might not hear from someone else because of the delicate nature of the knowledge. There have been assignments God has called me into where He said, "I'm going to need you to go in, teach these things, expose what is happening here, and then leave." He has gifted me to do this in a way that honors the people involved while exposing the intentions that are not honorable. So now I've learned to ask the Holy Spirit, "Is this a short assignment or a long one?" I've learned to accept that at times the assignment is not intended to result in me making a lot of friends, but rather in exposing how the enemy's strategies are operating so that change can occur.

Apostles' assignments will often be focused on breaking through, tearing down, and building or rebuilding. If you are a prophet, you will be speaking truth and organizing people into their places. If you are an evangelist, you will be promoting something. Teachers will be teaching others, and pastors will be caring for people. As you get to know the spiritual leader in you, you will begin to recognize these types of assignments. So now take the authority you have been given in your assignments, add to it your area of influence, and then one or more of the purposes that God calls believers to such as unity or healing or setting people free, or feeding the hungry, and you should start to see what your leadership assignments already do or will start to look like. But in order for you to become better equipped with discernment to tell the difference between an assignment from God to do His work or a strategy from the enemy to derail you, you have to become experienced in it and recognize the things that God would and wouldn't do, the way He would speak to you and the types of assignments He would call you into. There have been times when the Holy Spirit told me in my gut not to do something, but I ignored the warnings, and I definitely didn't check it against the Word.

So, how do you begin to develop your discernment in what to say yes to and what to say no to? The first helpful principle is to understand that the places God will often call you will be consistent with your hardwired spiritual gifts, not necessarily your skills and talents, in an area of influence or geographic area you have already been in. *Assignments* on the other hand, aren't necessarily lined up with your gifts. I have a friend who is apostolic and who is skilled in organizational development. She worked in the government sector her whole life, and just as she was preparing for retirement, God opened a door for her to begin to develop leadership training for high-level leaders within the governmental offices. When she developed the training, she used all of God's best practices in the training without quoting Scripture, and when people came to her and shared how impactful her training was, she was often able to share her faith with them. She knew by the personal way God orchestrated the assignment that it was Him and that in this case she was supposed to say yes, and that it was also consistent with her calling. Conversely, I was in a meeting with educators who were trying to build an initiative to launch where I quickly discerned that me being there was not consistent with my spiritual gifts. Though I was able to use my gifts to help them, I knew fairly quickly that this was an assignment, not a calling. Think of assignments as you are being a part of someone else's calling, whereas calling is uniquely designed for you to lead. I can now look back on many great things that I said yes to that did not end well, because I wasn't supposed to say yes to taking the lead to it as a calling, but instead as a contributor in an assignment.

Leadership is established when you are able to go through a refinement process with God and He nurtures your identity and purpose to align with His will. One positive to some of the obstacles that women face in leadership is that we get to go through the refining fire, almost as a given. But that is not the case for men necessarily because they are recognized in leadership as part of the cultural norm. Regardless, now that you have seen the steps God took me through for healing, and hopefully you have also begun to restore your power in Him, it's time to step into your kingdom calling. As you do, your journey will turn into testimony, and you will help reconcile others to Jesus as He has done for you. Your worldly truths will turn into a worldview that is aligned with Gods will for both you and the world. Your ministry will be unleashed as God anoints you to fully step into your anointing, and you will design blueprints that are consistent with God's design. And all of these things will be established as you partner with others in the Church in Unity.

Reflection

1. What has God done with you to help you restore things that have been lost from past experiences?
2. What is your calling or mantle?
3. What is your preferred message and way God uses you to preach it?
4. What ideas have you been able to create as you have let go of past baggage?
5. Do you feel like you have been refined by fire? If yes, how?

CHAPTER 16

THE POWER OF HER KINGDOM CALLING

"Then Jesus came to them and said, 'All authority in heaven and on earth has been given to me. Therefore go and make disciples of all nations, baptizing them in the name of the Father and of the Son and of the Holy Spirit, and teaching them to obey everything I have commanded you. And surely, I am with you always, to the very end of the age.'"

—MATTHEW 28:18–20

The final component of the P.I.N.K. framework is your Kingdom calling, which begins the season of your worldview being focused on God's Kingdom worldview. Some of the ways you will begin to operate in this new outlook will be the ministry of reconciliation, the building of ecosystems to help the Church work together in ministry better, beginning to create kingdom-focused solutions and blueprints, and receiving the anointing from God to fully recognize your mantles and calling. All of these things require the Church to help you with them and Unity is the way to see it come to fruition.

If you're like me, it might be hard to imagine what to do next. God has restored your identity, purpose, and leadership, but now what? Do you really believe He will restore it all? When God met me in the shower and asked me to write this book, I knew that he would not ask me to do that unless He was going to not only fully restore me, but that He would shift the Church. Isaiah 43:19 says, "See, I am doing a new thing! Now it springs up; do you not perceive it? I am making a way in the wilderness and streams in the wasteland." So, as we move into the final components of the P.I.N.K. Framework we have to let go of the old and begin to embrace the new. God is doing a new thing.

In the quiet town of Bethany, a small but resilient community gathered in a humble church. For years, the narratives within the church had focused on the male figures of the Bible, relegating women to supporting roles in both the church and culture. But change was on the horizon, and it started with the discovery of an old manuscript tucked away in the church's dusty archives. The manuscript contained forgotten stories of women in the Bible whose complexities and strengths had been overshadowed over time. As the church members delved into these narratives, they found a tapestry of courage, wisdom, and determination that challenged traditional perceptions. One woman, Lydia, emerged as a beacon of strength. She was not merely a seller of purple cloth but a savvy businesswoman who created opportunities for her community. Her open heart and home became a sanctuary for weary travelers, where profound discussions about faith and life took place. Another figure, Deborah, showcased unyielding leadership. She was not just a judge but a strategist who united her people to overcome adversity. Her wisdom and foresight led her to make bold decisions that transformed her society and reshaped history. The story of Phoebe unveiled a woman of influence. She was more than a servant; she was a respected deacon who demonstrated empathy and dedication, bridging gaps within the church community, and offering solace to the downtrodden.

As these narratives were shared with the congregation, perspectives shifted. The church members realized that women in the Bible were not merely side characters but central figures who demonstrated strength, faith, and leadership. Inspired by these stories, the church decided to incorporate these voices into their teachings and services. Over time, women in the congregation began to step into leadership roles that had been traditionally held by men. The pastor, recognizing the importance of men and women being co-heirs in God's kingdom, embraced this transformation and encouraged a more inclusive interpretation of the Bible's teachings. The church's revival brought a renewed sense of community, where everyone's strengths were celebrated regardless of gender. Men and women worked together to serve their town, carrying out projects that improved the lives of the less fortunate. The church's transformation resonated beyond Bethany. Other congregations took note, inspired to reexamine their own interpretations of Bible stories and the roles of women within their faith communities. In the end, the quiet church in Bethany became a testament to the power of revisiting narratives and recognizing the complexities and strengths of women in the Bible. As the congregation embraced a more inclusive view, they found that their faith grew richer, and their community became stronger than ever before.

The story above was written with the help of artificial intelligence (AI). If you're not familiar with artificial intelligence, it pulls from all the information that exists on the internet and gives the best explanation for an outcome, based on the questions you ask of it. Think of it as surveying the internet. Clearly the story is fiction, at the same time, there is truth to it, much like a worldview. A worldview is a collection of attitudes, values, and expectations about the world around us that informs our actions. Because much of the world is driven by a mainly patriarchal worldview, we are seeing the consequences of that imbalance, especially in women's issues. But to bring the fullness of God's kingdom worldview to fruition on earth as it is in heaven, we have to have a feminine worldview that complements the masculine. We need the women's perspective, especially in areas where women are the victims. Women have a unique ability to see the good in others and help bring it out. In the same way, it's how we see the world, people, and possibilities. And whether we recognize it or not, as women in America we carry a responsibility to help women in other countries who depend on us to lead the way, not only in freedom but in innovation, advocacy and solutions affecting women. Women of faith need to take our place at the tables, both governing and collaborative ones, around women's issues and movements. But it will take women and men together to change the world!

The first component of your Kingdom calling is the ministry of reconciliation. In 2 Corinthians 5:16-21, "So from now on we regard no one from a worldly point of view. Though we once regarded Christ in this way, we do so no longer. Therefore, if anyone is in Christ, the new creation has come. The old has gone, the new is here! All this is from God, who reconciled us to himself through Christ and gave us the ministry of reconciliation: that God was reconciling the world to himself in Christ, not counting people's sins against them. And he has committed to us the message of reconciliation. We are therefore Christ's ambassadors, as though God were making his appeal through us. We implore you on Christ's behalf: Be reconciled to God. God made him who had no sin to be sin for us, so that in him we might become the righteousness of God." We are all called to help people reconcile to Jesus. And our voice and message is first and foremost, that we are all reconciled to Him and He is not counting our sins against us.

At the same time, reconciling Scripture, the lies versus the truth, the attacks, and the shutdown of your voice and leadership, must also be reconciled. When people who don't know Jesus walk away from Him because of the way that the church acts towards them, that is not what God ever ordained. When it comes to the limiting belief system, and the message by many churches that women are less than and cannot lead, first it's not the truth, but second, it is keeping women in bondage and believing God has rejected them. We have to help reconcile this for others. God wants the whole Church engaged.

The second component of your calling is influencing others worldview through the building of ecosystems of people around you focused on similar calling and equip and empower those around you to become established in their identity, purpose, leadership, and kingdom calling. An ecosystem, according to Wikipedia, is a complex network or an interconnected system that is necessary to build and maintain an environment. In biology and in God's creation, for example, we know that the ocean is its own ecosystem and that God created it separately from the land, which is also an ecosystem. In the entrepreneurial world, ecosystem building is a term that means all the organizations and people necessary to fuel and sustain innovation. The ecosystem approach can be seen further in relation to the body of Christ and defines how we as women were meant to operate interdependently, not just with men but with all believers. In other words, we need each other. Scripture describes one version of an ecosystem in 1 Corinthians 12:12–27 like this,

> Just as a body, though one, has many parts, but all its many parts forms one body, so it is with Christ. For we were all baptized by one Spirit so as to form one body—whether Jews or Gentiles, slave or free—and we were all given the one Spirit to drink. Even so the body is not made up of one part but of many. Now if the foot should say, "Because I am not a hand, I do not belong to the body," it would not for that reason stop being part of the body. And if the ear should say, "Because I am not an eye, I do not belong to the body," it would not for that reason stop being part of the

body. If the whole body were an eye, where would the sense of hearing be? If the whole body were an ear, where would the sense of smell be? But in fact God has placed the parts in the body, every one of them, just as he wanted them to be. If they were all one part, where would the body be? As it is, there are many parts, but one body. The eye cannot say to the hand, "I don't need you!" And the head cannot say to the feet, "I don't need you!" On the contrary, those parts of the body that seem to be weaker are indispensable, and the parts that we think are less honorable we treat with special honor. And the parts that are unpresentable are treated with special modesty, while our presentable parts need no special treatment. But God has put the body together, giving greater honor to the parts that lacked it, so that there should be no division in the body, but that its parts should have equal concern for each other. If one part suffers, every part suffers with it; if one part is honored, every part rejoices with it. Now you are the body of Christ, and each one of you is a part of it.

God never intended for the Church to operate with one point of leadership who heard God better than everyone else. In fact, that is exactly how the old covenant operated but the new covenant is a team approach – the body of Christ. An ecosystem relies on *all* members of the system to do their part. In biology, when part of the ecosystem is changed or eliminated, at minimum the ecosystem is changed but it can also cause it to collapse. Conversely, while the ecosystem can remain operating when all of its participants are not present even if it's not optimal, when each member is doing its part and operating fully in its function, it causes the ecosystem to flourish. The body of Christ is not operating in its fullness without women!

The third component of your calling is the power to create your own blueprints in partnership with God to create something that only you can do, together with Him. A blueprint is a plan, or a design and the Kingdom is the fulfillment on earth of God's will. Regardless of the warfare and limiting behaviors that you may experience, God will continue to download ideas and blueprints to you that represent the fullness of His kingdom. Wholistic solutions require an ecosystem of people to execute. But instead of executing them right away, tuck them away and wait on God to direct your steps and bring the people needed to see it come to its fullness with Him. What I now know is that He first had to heal me for me to be able to see and hear better from Him, but then He had to train me to know what ideas to chase and what ideas to let go, like He will do for you. As you become well versed in some of His own blueprints, principles, and outcomes for building, like creation, reconciliation, setting the oppressed free, the fruit of the Spirit, putting on the armor of God, conflict resolution, and unity, you too will develop His plans.

At some point towards the end of my ministry journey, I was fortunate to get to visit a ministry that has discipled both men and women for over fifty years; they do these things I'm talking about well. They invite leaders from around the world to America and equip them to go back to their nations and share these same principles with other leaders, both male and female, in a way that multiplies their efforts 100 times for every leader they train.[14] During one of our visits, the women, who are discipled separately from the men, were presented with their graduation certificates, and had an opportunity to speak. I and other women leaders from the United States had spent our last week of school with the women and had gotten to know them, so they knew we were from America. One after one, they thanked the organization for the teaching, and they prayed over those of us in America, that we would begin to understand how free we are and how much our freedoms help other women in the world. They were pleading with us to understand this. These women leaders from around the world literally risk their lives for Jesus every day. And their prayers were that women in America would stand up and use their freedom to help other women around the world who are still fighting to be free. I'll never forget the experience. The Holy Spirit convicted me that day that we take our freedom for granted. God's blueprints are focused on all of His creation, believers, and non-believers, and are focused on the whole person, His whole Truth in Scripture, and His whole Church. And He is the Master Builder in His plans that He desires for each of us to be a part of.

So, how do you know what your part in His plan is? And how do you know that it is from God and that He has placed it in you? First, just like when you would build a house, you have to start with the infrastructure. The infrastructure is made up of your identity and purpose. What evidence can you see from your journey? Your truths? Your design? What is the Holy Spirit saying? What fivefold gift best describes how you are hardwired to do things? And are there any significant events in culture or in your family that mark a time frame that is important to you? Then, what natural talents and experiences do you have that you've learned that bring you energy? Add to that the spiritual gifts that you most often use and any lessons that you have learned or skills you have developed around spiritual warfare. All of these things that make up your personal identity and purpose are the structural pages of your blueprint. Next, add to those things the areas of culture you find yourself in most, the mantles and as-signments you feel like God gives you, what type of encounters with God you have had, and the things that were restored. Those things that caused you the most pain are often the place God will call you to bring solutions to. What is your testimony? What ecosystem of people are around you? What area of reconciliation has God defined in you? What blueprints are in you that you can't let go of?

The final component of your calling is that God gives you the anointing to finish what your started. God designed His people to work together, men and women, but He will give you something to lead, innovate and create with Him. Just because you don't lead at work or at home even, doesn't mean that God doesn't call you to lead. There is a leader in each of us. And God will both mantle and anoint you to lead in His kingdom plan. Part of God's plan is to set the oppressed free and Isaiah 58:6-12 He shows us, at least partially, how to do that,

Is not this the kind of fasting I have chosen: to loose the chains of injustice and untie the cords of the yoke, to set the oppressed free and break every yoke? Is it not to share your food with the hungry and to provide the poor wanderer with shelter when you see the naked, to clothe them, and not to turn away from your own flesh and blood? Then your light will break forth like the dawn, and your healing will quickly appear; then your righteousness will go before you, and the glory of the Lord will be your rear guard. Then you will call, and the Lord will answer; you will cry for help, and he will say: Here am I. If you do away with the yoke of oppression, with the pointing finger and malicious talk. and if you spend yourselves on behalf of the hungry and satisfy the needs of the oppressed, then your light will rise in the darkness, and your night will become like the noonday. The Lord will guide you always; he will satisfy your needs in a sun scorched land and will strengthen your frame. You will be like a well-watered garden, like a spring whose waters never fail. Your people will rebuild the ancient ruins and will raise up the age-old foundations; you will be called Repairer of Broken Walls, Restorer of Streets with Dwellings.

Street ministry was something I had never experienced before. Sex trafficking was definitely on the forefront of our minds in the beginning of the nonprofit ministry. One night we went out on the "track" in Sacramento where women are lined up on the streets for men to purchase sexual acts from, and we engaged the young girls who stood in line waiting for a man to drive up and pay for her services. That night was no different from any other, except the leader of the ministry had called me and asked if I would go with her to talk to a young lady having difficulty after giving birth to a baby boy after an emergency C-section. We walked into the hospital room, and it was as if I had known this girl my whole life. She was the same age as our oldest daughter. The nurses had not given her any medication after her birth, and she was in pain. I was able to get her what she needed from the nurses. That night began another part of our family's journey, as we were introduced to a future spiritual daughter and two godchildren. It also was the beginning of opening up our world to one of the most heinous crimes against women being perpetuated today. Of course, it was not only happening to girls, but it was mostly a crime against girls by men. God would continue to have me encounter women who had experienced trauma at the hands of men, from harassment to emotional and physical trauma and other crimes. Our family found ourselves helping this woman hide from her aggressor for a few years. At one point, while she was still in the hospital, someone from the church put a picture of her and her children on social media. Within minutes her former pimp was at the hospital asking for her. The evil men and women exploiting these children, mostly girls, knew psychologically what it took to groom them so they would never be free from their abusers. They would seek them out, find them where they were, and entice them through the control they continued to have over the children that they shared with the ladies for the rest of their lives.

As our family grew close to this young woman and walked with her through her healing, she would ask us why Jesus would allow this abuse and how Jesus could be real if this is the way He operated. No one had ever told her that what these boys did to her was not okay. She just needed to hear that it was not how it was supposed to be and not something that Jesus wanted for her. After continuing to be pursued by these pimps, she eventually succumbed to their control and became caught up in an abusive relationship. Ultimately, as of the printing of this book, she has not been able to break free. I often wonder if there was more that we could have done or could do today. But honestly, it felt like at every turn there were not enough organizations, money, professionals, and willingness of others to help her with everything she needed to restore her back to who God designed her to be.

"We dream of a day when homelessness has an answer, where there are no more kids in foster care, where sexual exploitation and broken relationships are replaced with loving, Christ-centered marriages, where poverty is a choice, where racism is overwhelmed by love, where Christians and the Church are seen as the answer, not the problem, and where God is worshiped openly in public again."

This was the vision statement of the nonprofit ministry I founded and led. It still moves me today. But I've realized this vision will never be recognized without the whole Church. The whole Church includes men and women, every ethnicity, every culture, every nation in the world. The whole Church is the entire body of Christ, all believers of Jesus working together, honoring each other, and understanding how and why God designed them and their unique purpose. I pray we get there. I know that God is doing a new thing and that this is what He wants to do. The culture is crying out for it. The Church is listening and hearing His voice in it. We're seeing the evidence of God doing it. And I now know that while I or others in ministry are not her savior and that only God is, He will anoint me, you, and others, to eventually restore her to Him. I pray I get to be a part of that or at least witness it in my lifetime.

It matters to God if we are silent! The world is looking to us to lead the way. Culture has shifted into a world that is demanding that women and people of diverse ethnicities be recognized and honored. And while much of this truth has been politicized to gain power, the shift has still happened. We are not going back. Additionally, the leading driver of political movements today is social movements! Social movements are leading and demanding change in various areas of society, not just in the United States but in the world. Unfortunately, the Christian worldview is largely missing from these movements except to say that we need to go back to the way it was. Women, including Christian women whether they are proclaiming it loudly or not, are not going back. In areas like sexuality, abortion, healthy families and marriages, health care, business, the arts, media, entertainment, the culture is responding to the change. There is an explosion of social influence being led by women and ethnically diverse voices. And there is a lot of talk about unity. God is the only one who knows what each of us individually and corporately needs to transform culture in this season.

Women of faith are not only part of the social movements today, but we are also not represented in culture's view of womanhood today. We do not march for feminism mainly because we have been taught to remain silent, but we also choose to remain silent! The world knows that if we were to start showing up as women of faith, we would not be able to condone some of the things that women are expected to accept, so we often are told not to come. Are we going to let the world march for and raise our children? Or is it time that we raise our voices and refuse to acquiesce any longer to the pressure? While we have been on the sidelines and systematically shut down, evil has been prevailing. And frankly, the false doctrines of the old covenant of slavery, female submission, and male domination are fueling some of these outcomes. If this is what God ordained, then why are His outcomes not present? I regularly ask Jesus how he would want us to respond to a particular issue in the world today and His answer is always the same, Love. How did He respond? He demonstrated love by supernaturally walking in their shoes, having compassion on them, pointing out their sin in love, healing them and then empowering them with His Spirit to go and sin no more.

According to Fortune.com[15], in 2023, 29 of the fortune 500 businesses are led by female CEOs. That's up 20% from last year's 24 female chief executives, for a total share of 5.8%. The Global 500 trails the Fortune 500, where women now run 10.4% of businesses.

While females comprise nearly half of all entry-level positions, their numbers decrease substantially the higher they go up the organization ladder. The reasons often cited for a lack of gender diversity include women's greater tendency to sacrifice career for family, conscious and unconscious bias, and a lack of mentorship opportunities. Looking at similar statistics from pewresearch.com, the numbers in churches are even worse. In the United States today, most church denominations have limits to the authority they will give to women in the institutional church setting. According to www.pewresearch.org, 49 percent of the world's population are women, 72 percent of women identify as Christians, 60 percent of women work in the workforce which includes the church, but only 31 percent are business owners.[16]

Though some denominations and even nondenominational pastors say they "accept" women in leadership and in all positions of the church, the reality is the evidence tells a different story. Some of that can be explained by understanding the definitions of acceptance of women in leadership, such as complementarianism (only support roles to women) versus egalitarianism (all roles to women). Additionally, 80 percent of pastors are men, and of the 20 percent of women who are pastors, 70 percent of those women pastors are unpaid and only 2 percent are in a leadership position (outside of pastoring) in a church. This means that though 50 percent of churches claim they are complementarian, the evidence suggests the real number of churches and people who believe women can only lead in support roles must be higher, even if it is an unintended injustice.

Another interesting statistic from pewresearch.com is that while 69 percent of women absolutely believe in God, only 59 percent believe that religion is important, only 40 percent attend church weekly, 33 percent once or twice a month or a few times a year, and 26 percent never. It appears that statistics support that women are choosing to sit out of churches, at least for a season.[17]

God never intended for us to sit on the sidelines. If you are, I hope I have been able to give you hope and consider otherwise. I pray that God, the Holy Spirit, and Jesus, will meet you in three distinct ways, to heal you and give you hope for your future. As bad as you think your story might be, God is a God of redemption and restoration. He will get you through to the end if you are able to stick it out. We are all necessary in God's plan, and He not only needs us all to step into our calling, but He designs our calling so we will need others to fulfill His plans. We cannot do it alone. So, if the Church is not our ecosystem, who is?

Reflection

1. Why is unity important to God?
2. What makes up your worldview?
3. What would a movement of Jesus-loving women look like?
4. What power to change the world have women acquiesced to men?
5. Does the word *feminism* scare you? Why? Have you ever looked at the definition or have you only heard it from others? How is feminism different from the feminist movement?

CONCLUSION

Thank you for going on this journey with me and congratulations on getting to the end of this process, whether it marks the beginning, end or somewhere in between of your own journey! My prayer is that you have begun to rediscover who you are as a woman in the eyes of Jesus and are allowing Him to restore His power through you. I hope that this book has been and will continue to be helpful to your own journey to freedom. Restoration takes time and starts with the truth. And the truth is that many leaders in the Church have intentionally set out to disrupt the identity, purpose, leadership, and calling of women. They've done this by partnering with culture and politics to extend a few limiting beliefs about the Scriptures to justify bad behavior, keep women from becoming established in leadership positions in both the Church and culture, and systematically shutting down our voices. If you are a woman, especially in leadership who is passionate about Jesus, this is the moment we stop accepting less than. It's time to start walking in the freedom that God's designed in us as part of His plan. Instead of whispering under our breath, sharing our frustrations discreetly, rolling our eyes at disparaging or degrading comments, and crying together when the promotions don't come, it's time to do something about it. And it's not just about us. It's about our daughters, granddaughters, sisters, and women around the world who are directly affected by our choices. And it's about our men, too, and the Church itself where half of God's coheirs are sitting on the sidelines. It's time for unity in the Church, and it cannot happen until God's daughters' step into position.

As God took me and you on a journey with Him, He has helped us see the truth. He has shown us that conservative churches and denominations did previously ordain and commission women in pastoral positions in churches and that there was a change in the 1980s to remove that authority. And as a response to the women's movement of the 1960's and the influx of women wanting to be pastors in the 1970's, in a secret meeting of men only, a new term was coined that mandates limitations for women in the churches and even defines roles for women as homemakers while men are free to lead in culture. He also has helped us see that those changes were codified through politics and political action committees by using terms like "family values" to further the agenda. But He also wanted us to see in His Word that Jesus did and does advocate on women's behalf, supports our freedom and our causes, stands with us in our battles, defends our children, and desires to shift culture on our behalf. And He revealed His desire for women to help Him restore other women to the Church so that we can see ourselves there, in sermons, discipleship programs, and leadership trainings, as well as in the way churches engage in culture. He wants to correct the lies we have been told and have accepted, and He revealed to us through the PINK framework that Personal identity, Incubated purpose, Nurtured leadership, and Kingdom calling results in peace and freedom. And then He restored our prophetic voice and helped us, begin to dream again through innovation and entrepreneurship as we explored building our own kingdom blueprints, that we can pass down as part of our own spiritual legacy. Finally, we cast vision for the future of women and the Church and God's desire to restore women.

Friends, men are not going to do this for us. Even if they could, it's not for them to do. It's time for us to raise our voices. The world depends on it. The Church is broken, and at the foundation of its brokenness is division. The fruit of the systematic shutdown of women is the loss of our children in the Church to culture. The branding of the enemy is a heart that will not reconcile, restore, and rebuke those who partner with sinful behavior and continue to target and take down those in the Church. But God is doing a new thing. He is not only restoring women, but He is shifting His Church. I started researching and writing this book in September 2021 and by early 2022 had the first draft completed but I was not healed enough yet and God had not released me to publish it yet. As much as this process was personal to me, I also knew that if God was going to restore women and shift the Church, He would do it through many, many people, and that my journey and book would be just one of many things He would do to create the shift. During that research and writing phase of the book, God highlighted to me a prophetic word that Charismanews.com[18] printed from Larry Sparks from July 1, 2017, the same time that God had told me a transition was coming. In his prophetic word, he started with this,

"In the spirit, I see the King of glory knighting women with swords, as if to authorize them to offensively advance the kingdom into spheres of society that demand solutions only Holy Spirit can provide. When men carry these solutions, half of the assignment is being accomplished—and that's great. But when the Spirit was poured out, men represented only half of the containers purposed to carry God's glory, power, and strategies into the earth; women are the missing link. I believe God's wonder women are the key to unlocking the fullness of outpouring into the earth, an outpouring that will only come to the world through the people of God."

On June 1, 2021, a local pastor from Roseville, California, and someone who I greatly respect, Lance Hahn, released a podcast following years of research around what God really wants when it comes to women in leadership in the church. In the podcast, *Understanding Women in Ministry, on the Lance Hahn Podcast*, Pastor Hahn admits that because of 1 Timothy 2:12, that says, "I do not permit a woman to teach or to assume authority over a man, she must be quiet" means that very few churches embrace women's voices at the pulpit or in the boardroom. But he also states that there is an argument that the *priesthood of all believers*, includes women in God's plan. And Lance concludes, after taking you through the scriptures, that women can preach and teach and that "we need a much better equity of voice" of women in churches. You can listen to his podcast and the conclusion of his research here.[19]

In January 2023, a prophet by the name of Jeremiah Johnson, released a word about a move of "fiery apostolic women" on YouTube. "God is raising up kingdom women who have blueprints", he says. "The power of witchcraft attacks will be broken off of you this year".[20] He went on to say that the enemy had orchestrated a "systematic shutdown" of women, the exact words God gave me. On July 6, 2023, Jeremiah Johnson was on a live Facebook show with Mike Signorelli, where the two of them came together and discussed what God is doing with women beginning in 2023.[21] Specifically, they discussed that God is raising up women in the marketplace and wanted them to know that they should "try again" those things that did now work the first time.

And finally, on June 7, 2023, Pastor Rick Warren, after being kicked out of the Southern Baptist Convention for ordaining women, issued an apology to all women. His sentiments are similar to others I have heard from so many men who took the time to research the Scriptures involving women and leadership and came to the same conclusion. I appreciate them all for their courage to take a stand. Without men standing up and locking arms with us, I fear women will have no choice but to go it alone, for longer than any of us want or God intends. This is not God's desire or design for any of us. Here's Pastor Warren's apology published June 7, 2023, on Facebook and Twitter:

My biggest regret in 53 years of ministry is that I didn't do my own personal exegesis sooner on the 4 passages used to restrict women. Shame on me.

I wasted those 4 yrs of Greek in college & seminary. When I finally did my proper "due diligence", laying aside 50 years of bias, I was shocked, chagrined, and embarrassed.

So many hermeneutical rules were being violated including Never build a doctrine on a single word that is used only once in scripture! There's nothing to compare it to (correlation.) Do your own study of authentein in ancient Greek and you'll be shocked too.

I think maybe it was because I didn't WANT to know anything that might challenge the view, I WANTED to believe for 50 yrs. But eventually, integrity required that I read over 70 commentaries by INERRANTIST scholars that blew apart my comfortable, traditional, and culture-based interpretation. No seminary told me that those commentaries even existed and Baptist Bookstores refused to carry them. (My mother managed a Baptist Bookstore.) So I accepted the interpretation that was most comfortable for me as a man with my background.

Then reading over 100 books on the early church and the history of the Great Commission (for FTT) demanded my repentance. That journey was both painful and humbling.

I don't expect to win in New Orleans, and I certainly don't expect to change the mind of any angry fundamentalist. They are responsible to God, not to me. I'm doing this as an act of obedience to the Holy Spirit.

But I DO want to do this: I PUBLICLY APOLOGIZE to every good woman in my life, church, and ministry that I failed to speak up for in my years of ignorance. What grieves me is that I hindered them in obeying the Great Commission command (And Acts 2:17–18) that EVERYONE is to TEACH in the church.

I held them back from using the spiritual gifts and leadership skills that the Holy Spirit had sovereignly placed in them. That breaks my heart now, and I am truly repentant and sorry for my sin. I wish I could do it all over. Christian women, will you please forgive me?

Regardless of attacks and the vote result, I want a clear conscience before my Master . . . that I repented, and that this sinner did what he asked me to do. With that I am completely content to let Him be the judge and evaluator of my life and ministry.

We must live for an Audience of One.

I can't tell you how much this apology and the timing of it means to me. It has taken me two years to write this book because I wasn't sure I wanted the hate that I knew would come from what I was concluding. And honestly, I needed the confirmation from healthy men of God too! Not just because I didn't want to lead anyone astray, but I also wanted to confirm God's timing. I care too much for Jesus and His Church. But everything God gave these men to say, and that Rick Warren wrote, validated what I discovered myself during my journey. And I am only one example of a woman who tried to walk out Gods calling and suffered the consequences of a broken system. There are so many more of us, and I have met many of them, and I'm guessing it includes many of you. It's time to try something else. I pray that not one more generation of women has to endure what we have endured. There's no way you can convince me that's what Jesus would have done.

I have spent a decent amount of time in this book detailing the specific things that women have experienced and the potential outcomes that we see in the Church and culture today as women and millennials especially are leaving the church. When the church restores women, the Church will be restored, and culture will follow. The messaging over a lifetime destroyed my identity, and maybe it has destroyed yours too. Identity disruption leads to bondage. And bondage leads to death, for both today and generations to come. How do we ensure this doesn't happen to our sons and daughters moving forward? We have to unwind this for the sake of our families and the Church and for the sake of Christ.

The Church should lead the way in restoring its culture to respect, honor, and support women equally as coheirs of God's kingdom. Awareness and truth are a good start, but we can also begin to ask more questions and expect more questions and more openness around the limiting belief system. And churches can start by posting where they stand on the limiting beliefs about women so that we can all see them for ourselves and make a more informed choice. In culture, we can start by using our voices to represent Jesus' worldview in us and begin to build a new operating system for women that reflects how God really loves us and wants us to be co-heirs in His plan. We can raise awareness about the importance of women in culture and be intentional about empowering women to tell their stories and share their experiences, while supporting their platforms and initiatives amplifying women's voices. And finally, let's create pathways for women to take on leadership roles in various areas of culture, encourage collaboration and discipleship; and be intentional about committing to long-term strategies that are sustainable and represent Jesus to the world.

Unity is a diverse people, speaking with diverse sounds, woven together to show the world God is alive and loves them, with one collective voice derived from many established voices.

JESUS
IN BLUE

"He gives strength to the weary and increases the power of the weak. Even youths grow tired and weary, and young men stumble and fall; but those who hope in the LORD will renew their strength. They will soar on wings like eagles; they will run and not grow weary; they will walk and not be faint."

—ISAIAH 40:29–31

The greatest power of the Church comes when men and women are together. Pride causes men to refuse to listen, to see what's in front of them, and to have a conversation about the issues. Submission and control are the helpers of pride. If you never have to confront your issues, then you can continue to grow in them. Positions and titles have become your idols. Men, put on your armor and help us free women once and for all!

I almost finished this book without writing this chapter—mostly because, obviously, this book is primarily a message for women. But God exhorted me to speak to men as well. Along the way in my experience, for every man who shut me down, there were men who didn't. I wouldn't say there were ever a substantial number of men who stood next to me, defended me, or championed me, but there were some, including my husband. At the same time, I was in such a place of brokenness over some of the more egregious abuses that occurred at the hands of men at times in my life, I'm not sure I could have received it from them anyway.

Imagine what would happen if men and women of the Church were acting in concert with each other. How beautiful and what an expression of the fullness of God we would be demonstrating for the world! In the same way that many women lament the way the Church has oppressed their roles and callings, there are many men who also feel their identities are not represented in the Church either. Men in business, for example, often lament that they are only called on for money and not for purposes in the church. Men who do not fit the "warrior" identity bucket also often feel like they don't fit. My husband is one of those men! We sat in the same church for fifteen years where I was offered many roles to start and launch ministries in the church. And while my husband was acknowledged for being my "helper," he was ironically one of the only men of the original founding families of the church who was never asked to be a leader in any way. He was never asked to be an elder or teacher or even a deacon. Why? Because he didn't fit the mold.

My husband has championed me for thirty-five years, sometimes better than I deserved. God knew what He would eventually ask me to do in life, and He gave me the best man to partner with for the job. My husband doesn't care what the world thinks of him, like I have of myself in the past. But he really loves and cares about me. And God has used him over the years to give me Godly perspective and support that the Father in heaven would give. And along the way,

God also showed me how to love him back and how men are wired and how in my passion for life I could also change the course of his life, in good ways and bad. God has guided us both in how to walk out marriage as one unit, an ecosystem of family, where at times he took more of the burden in certain areas than I did and vice versa. God also met us in raising our children, all daughters, and now our grandchildren, each of us giving the best of what God designed in us and learning not only to accept but to celebrate the things that we love about each other as well as the things that drive us crazy about each other, because we're very different in every way! He's a teacher, soft and gentle in his approach, and we complement each other. Not because we chose the perfect person solely because of the complement, but because, in refining each other, we became One.

Men, you, too, are loved by both God and women. We love that you make us feel safe, that you are strong, and that you focus on one thing and do it. We love that you love us well and that you love our daughters and sons and mothers and fathers well. We love that you want to take on the burden of providing for your family and friends and that you want to protect us from life being a harsh reminder sometimes that we live in a world of sin. And we love that you want to love and honor God in all that He has designed you to be and do. And that you want to honor His Word as much as we do. But the world today has evolved and does not recognize women as less than and God needs us to respond. While past seasons required you to take the lead in physical wars and sacrifice, the season for today is more than that. God needs His entire Church together and activated. This has always been His design, but it hasn't always been the main focus of past seasons in the way it is now. So, would you help us become what God wants us to be? In the same way you help your mother, sister, aunt, grandmother, and daughters, let's help raise up the beautiful feminine voice of God. You understand this. You know what I'm saying is true. Let's do this together. Our sons and daughters need us.

So, what does that look like? First, you need as much healing as we do. In the Church, we still see the same number of divorces that the world does. We do not look different from the world. But we should if we believe Scripture. And we would if we understood who we are and how God designed us. Healthy male–female relationships are two-sided. It's how God designed us to be, coheirs together operating as a unit, as opposed to us operating individually and independently. He used marriage as the example of what those relationships should look like. Church tradition and the historical patriarchal societies that both Jewish and Christian traditions are steeped in perpetuated male-dominant, male-led cultures. Men have to understand that history matters. History repeats itself unless there is an intentional effort to change it. Women, by way of birthing children and life, get this instinctually. This does not seem to be the case for many men. It's much easier to keep doing the same thing when you are in the dominant position of power. It's incredibly comfortable. The injustice is glaring to everyone except the ones in the power positions.

Men, I'm praying you can hear this. The operating systems of the world were designed by you and continue to help you succeed. Conversely, they were not designed nor influenced by women. Jesus tried to demonstrate how to respond to this. If you are not looking through the lens of a woman in your life, you will only see it through your masculine lens. And your masculine lens is entrenched in all areas of culture, and the impact it is making on the world is placing women in bondage and servitude toward that lens. You personally may not feel like you have any mean-spirited intentions of bias toward women, but by continuing not to acknowledge your part and partnering with the masculine systems you built that carry your perspective only, you are playing a part. Being complacent and doing nothing is playing a part. And the part you are playing is destroying women, and the ramifications of those choices are destroying the Church.

When our oldest daughter started her first career job, I warned her of what she might face in the workplace. She looked at me and said,

"Mom, that doesn't exist anymore. People don't act or think that way in our generation." I replied to her, "You're right to an extent. But wait until you inadvertently find yourself having to stand up to the unwanted advances of a man in a power position and see what happens." Within two months of being at the company, she received a text message on her personal phone from a man in the company asking her if she would go out with him. This man turned out to be the head of security for the corporation, a successful financial firm, who had taken the initiative to look up her personal employment information so that he could ask her out. And while he didn't harass her into going out with him, the fact that he thought it was acceptable to break his own company's security protocol because he was in charge, is indicative of the belief systems that it's ok for men to push the limits despite the rules. She said no to him and wasn't at that company long enough to see if anything would have come from it. But, as a mom, I was hoping that she was right and that this kind of thinking had ended, I wanted to go in there and let him get a glimpse of this mama bear. But I didn't because I didn't have to. We have two strong daughters who know how to stand up for themselves.

Men, when women come to you and tell you what is happening to them at the hands of other men, you have to listen, and you have to use discernment but hear them and believe them. And if you can't do that, you really need to search yourself in partnership with the Holy Spirit and ask why you don't! If a man came to you and told you that something tragic had just happened to him, you would believe him. When it's a woman and you refuse to acknowledge the oppression against them, you are an accessory to it! Just because you believe that you have no bias in you and that you would not act that way does not mean that every man is the same as you. And when you protect those men in your churches, businesses, and families instead of defending your wives, daughters, and other women, you might as well be the one committing the abuse. Generational abuse and trauma do not go away just because laws change. Laws don't change behavior; they just cause the behavior to go underground. Only God can change the hearts of men. If you are a man, this is how you can help:

1. Listen, pray, and seek God on what you may have a hard time hearing, seeing, and knowing when others tell you things that feel contrary to what you think.
2. Have empathy and try to understand what it is like to walk in someone else's shoes.
3. Stop blaming women for everything. When you blame us for the way we look and how that causes you to stumble, you are negating your own power and your own sin. I'm not saying we shouldn't consider you when we do things, but I am saying you should start considering us when you condone your actions as well.
4. We are qualified. Let's just start being honest here. We've been doing the work for so long in all areas, and yet men get the titles. A title does not qualify you. Doing the work does. So, stop saying we are not qualified because we haven't had the title.
5. Stop stealing our ideas, projects, and initiatives. God created you to be unique and divine in your own accord. Come up with your own ideas or partner with women in a healthy way. But stop taking our ideas and making them your own.
6. Stop using the Bible to reject us in Jesus's name. It's hurtful, and it's a stumbling block to your own faith. You will be held to a high standard for this.
7. Stop making us a token to make you look good! Women can spot this from a mile away, and it doesn't help you. We must be fully integrated into the team, not just put at the pulpit occasionally to make it look like you're including us. When you try to portray that you're inclusive of women and non-white ethnicities but it's only for show, you send a message that you and your entire organization lack integrity.
8. Start verbalizing your beliefs regarding complementarianism versus egalitarianism. If you believe it, then say it! Stop using it

to make people believe you affirm women without limits when you don't.

9. Start paying us what you are paid to do similar work.
10. Start passing the baton to and sharing leadership positions with women.
11. Start empowering us to write our own books about women. Women should be experts about women.
12. Include our perspective in decision making, strategy development, and Bible teaching. We need to see ourselves in the Bible! Stop always saying he and include her. And start preaching about the women in the Bible as leaders instead of only being there because men didn't do their job. This causes so much damage.
13. Support women-initiated ministries, research, businesses, innovation, and creativity fully so that the gap in funding can be fully recognized. You are in the power positions from both a leadership perspective and a financial perspective. You hold the power to change the world or oppress it.

Remember, these things make up what and how women need to be supported to make up for lost time in leadership. Women need education, a network, exposure, experience, opportunity, mentoring, the ability to be part of and have a voice in innovation, the funding to start and grow endeavors, and finally, the ability and platform to have a seat at the table with a voice that is honored for what it brings.

APPENDIX A

Resources

Recommended Books

- Paul, Women and Wives, Craig S. Keener,
- How I Changed My Mind about Women in Leadership, Alan F. Johnson, 2010
- Fashioned to Reign, Empowering Women to Fulfill their Divine Destiny, Kris Valloton
- The Prophets Manual, John Eckhart
- The Apostles Manual, John Eckhart
- Bible Women, Lindsay Hardin Freeman
- Pigs in the Parlor, Frank, and Ida Mae Hammond
- Jesus and John Wayne, Kristin Kobes Du Mez

Recommended Websites

- Ryan LeStrange.com
- gallup.com (Clifton Strengths)
- destinyfinder.com
- spiritualgifts.com
- 5lovelanguages.com

Fivefold Ministry Assessment Questions

Apostle

- Do you find yourself wanting to help people discover who they are?
- Do you see the way things should be?
- Are the steps to a solution often obvious to you?
- Do you often just know things?
- Are you frustrated when others can't understand the same things?
- Are you able to see the potential in people?
- Does it bring you great joy to be able to inspire others in seeing what they cannot see in themselves? Conversely, does it frustrate you that they remain stuck?
- Do you often find yourself walking with them in their journey and enjoy their victories?
- Do you often have a running dialogue of critiques going on in your mind when seeing a situation?
- Are you often frustrated because you spend an inordinate amount of time pouring into others and they do not reciprocate?
- Do you spend time trying to fix things? Or trying to solve problems?

Prophet

- Does God often ask you to reveal the heart of God for people?
- Does God give you prophetic dreams and words for people about themselves or things?
- Does God show you injustice and how to speak encouragement into it?
- Do you find yourself compelled to help the needy, broken and oppressed?

- Are you easily distracted by what seems like random thoughts, ideas, words, and pictures?
- Do you have strong feelings for whether something is from God or not?
- Do you believe life is about choices and you can choose your destiny?
- Do you frequently get gut feelings and are usually right about your opinions?
- Do you feel, understand, and relate to God's heart for people when you pray for them?
- Are you able to discern spirits?
- Do you see demons? Angels?
- Do you often find yourself giving directional steps to leaders?

Evangelist

- Do you love to share the good news?
- Do you enjoy celebrating people's transformation?
- Do you often play a significant role inviting people into God's family?
- Is it important to you to have friends, relationships, and a life outside your church? circle.
- Are you able to get other people excited about what you are excited about?
- Are highly adaptable and feel comfortable in almost any setting you are in?
- Do you have a heart for people who are far from God?
- Do you make other people feel comfortable when you are around?
- Do you feel frustrated when church is more inward focused than outward focused?
- Do you REALLY love the things you love?
- Are you intentional and strategic before you open your mouth and say something?
- Are you convinced that God is good?

- Do you believe your life should speak louder than your words?
- Do you speak boldly and speak your mind? So much so that it sometimes catches people off guard?
- Do you get excited when eyes are upon you?

Pastor

- Do you have compassion towards people and want to be sure they are cared for?
- Do you enjoy including and connecting with people?
- Do you consider yourself a good listener?
- Do you often council people?
- Have you facilitated supernatural healing and restoration in people?

Teacher

- Do you feel a responsibility to protect the Bible and the interpretation of it?
- Do you enjoy making complex issues easy to understand?
- Do you have a unique ability to help people apply scriptures to their life?
- Does memorizing scripture come easy for you?

ABOUT
THE AUTHOR

Tamera Vallejo is a mother, daughter, Mimi, wife, entrepreneur, professor, and lover of Jesus. She currently resides in California and is passionate about leadership and entrepreneurship as key strategies to restore women and unleash the Church to be the best version of itself. Tamera writes based on her extensive experiences in church, business, real estate, education, nonprofits, and startups and in innovation, systems, and leadership development as an executive leader, founder, broker, and CEO.

Tamera is gifted with a strong apostolic call and has ministered throughout the United States. She has extensive experience in equipping churches, businesses, and cities to recognize, empower and unleash the body of Christ into teams that more effectively minister to and set the oppressed free. She is a true pioneer and entrepreneur developing multiple strategies with biblical outcomes that are targeted on spiritual wholeness and bringing true freedom in Christ to the oppressed.

Tamera Vallejo founded Jesus In Pink, a marketplace ministry for Women in Leadership, to become more established in their own

Kingdom Identity, Purpose, Leadership and Calling in 2021. After 15+ years in formal ministry Tamera recognized that true freedom through salvation could not be recognized without the attributes and gifts of the whole Church, specifically focusing on women in ministry. Tamera also founded *The Unleashed Church*, to equip and send out the body of Christ, and became a first time Author in 2024. Prior to transitioning into these new wineskin ministries, Tamera founded Real Estate with Purpose, a social impact real estate solution in 2005; the E49 Corporation in 2009 to unite churches to solve social issues; Suite 210 and The Creator's Place, hubs in the community in 2013 and 2019 respectively, where faith and commerce come together; along with multiple social impact solutions to homelessness, sex trafficking and poverty, including Compassion Village, a Tiny Home Community for people experiencing homelessness in 2017.

Along with her entrepreneurial endeavors, Tamera is a much sought after conference speaker and has developed hundreds of custom workshops and training programs, incubator, and accelerator programs, and seminars, in both corporate and church settings. As the founder of With Purpose, Inc, a social purpose accelerator focused on blending faith and commerce, she has extensive experience in training leadership teams in identity, purpose, leadership and calling, as well as, how to successfully inspire social entrepreneurs how to validate their ideas, launch their product or service and scale their companies.

Tamera also serves on the faculty of Jessup University in Rocklin, CA. She and her husband, have two children, and reside in the Sacramento area.

Start here, **www.jesusinpink.com**, for more resources.

There are a multitude of resources here to help you in your own journey of self-discovery and reconciliation. I don't know about you, but I wanted to read everything I could get my hands on after God opened me up to His truths! Once you have satisfied yourself through self-discovery in partnership with the Holy Spirit, or for those of you that are already there, you can access more extensive training on the PINK framework process including The PINK Hive, Institute, Mentoring Group Retreats focused on Identity/Purpose and Leadership/Calling modules, as well as peer mentoring and one-on-one coaching, to help you establish your own your blueprint and walk alongside you as you step into your new pink lens!!!

Visit **tamerav.com** for a full list of her publications and her next series, The Unleashed Church. Using biblical principles and her own experiences in unity and setting the oppressed free, Tamera Vallejo offers a practical guide to understand how the body of Christ can more effectively minister together in churches, cities, regions, and nations. You'll discover how to shift the Church from a hierarchical leadership model to an empowering ecosystem model focused on equipping all believers to become more established in their own identity, purpose, leadership and calling. Take your ministry to a higher level of spiritual understanding and set people free.

Stay tuned for additional books in the Jesus In Pink and the Unleashed Church series'!

Endnotes

1 "The Danvers Statement," The Council on Biblical Manhood and Womanhood, CWMW.org, https://cbmw.org/about/danvers-statement/

2 "Resolution on Ordination and the Role of Women in Ministry," Southern Baptist Convention, SBC.org, June 1,1984, https://www.sbc.net/resource-library/resolutions/resolution-on-ordination-and-the-role-of-women-in-ministry/

3 Rick Warren, "My biggest regret in 53 years of ministry," Twitter.com, June 10, 2023, https://twitter.com/RickWarren/status/1667620086251925505?ref_src=twsrc%5Etfw%7Ctwcamp%5Etweetembed%7Ctwterm%5E1667620086251925505%7Ctwgr%5Effcd3944b23fdb02f1a32ea8b11d8ba9948fa30c%7Ctwcon%5Es1_&ref_url=https%3A%2F%2Fiframe.nbcnews.com%2Fn7SVfj4%3F_showcaption%3Dtrueapp%3D1

4 Jennifer LeClaire, The Deborah Anointing, Lake Mary, FL, Charisma House Book Group, 2015

5 "Making More of Women's Strengths, 40 Years After Title IX", news.gallup.com, https://news.gallup.com/opinion/gallup/170402/making-women-strengths-years-title.aspx/

6 Christianity.com accessed on 1/8/24.

7 Tom White, The Believers Guide to Spiritual Warfare, (Bloomington, MN., Chosen Books, 4/27/2011

8 Merriam Websters Dictionary accessed on 12/15/23, "fraternity".

9 Merriam Websters Dictionary accessed on 2/2/23, "apostle".

10 Merriam Websters Dictionary accessed on 2/2/23, "authority".

11 Merriam Webster Dictionary accessed on 2/2/23, "incubate".

12 Destinyfinder.com

13 Merriam Webster Dictionary accessed on 2/2/23, "innovation".

14 The Haggai Institute, https://www.haggai-international.org

15 Fortune.com, Meet the 29 female CEOs who run a record-high 5.8% of the companies on Fortune's Global 500 list. August 2, 2023, https://fortune.com/2023/08/02/fortune-global-500-female-ceos-women/#

16 Pewresearch.com, The Gender Gap in Religion Around the World, March 3, 2016, https://www.pewresearch.org/religion/2016/03/22/the-gender-gap-in-religion-around-the-world/

17 Pewresearch.com, Gender Composition, https://www.pewresearch.org/religion/religious-landscape-study/gender-composition/

18 Charismanews.com, Prophetic Word: God is Handing out Swords

and Mantles to His Wonder Women, Larry Sparks, July 1, 2017, https://www.charismanews.com/opinion/65889-prophetic-word-god-is-handing-out-swords-and-mantles-to-his-wonder-women

19 The Lance Hahn Podcast, Episode 39: Understanding Women in Ministry, June 1, 2021, https://www.accessmore.com/episode/Understanding-Women-in-Ministry-?fbclid=IwAR2hDRbnzrHeiZ7W55XLN7-54hd2J-VSNLlK-2gzeGaqWb1-gGaG4VZEwoeI/

20 Prophetic Word for Women, Jeremiah Johnson, January 2023, Youtube.com, https://www.youtube.com/watch?v=L6guhIfoqEM

21 Facebook Live, Mike Signorelli with Jeremiah Johnson, July 6, 2023 https://fb.watch/oVKw5w1aIJ/?mibextid=UVffzb&startTimeMs=177000